# Making Wooden FISHING LURES

## Carving and Painting Techniques that Really Catch Fish!

By Rich Rousseau

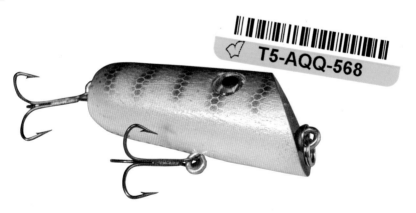

T5-AQQ-568

FOX CHAPEL
PUBLISHING

# Dedication

I would like to dedicate this book to Raymond "Boots" Smith. He was a good man to his family and his friends, and he was also my fishing partner. When Boots wasn't watching over his grandchildren and great-grandchildren, we spent many enjoyable hours in the fishing boat. I know he will save me a seat in his new boat; until then, I will miss him very much.

© 2010 by Rich Rousseau and Fox Chapel Publishing Company, Inc., East Petersburg, PA.

*Making Wooden Fishing Lures* is an original work, first published in 2010 by Fox Chapel Publishing Company, Inc. The patterns contained herein are copyrighted by the author. Readers may make copies of these patterns for personal use. The patterns themselves, however, are not to be duplicated for resale or distribution under any circumstances. Any such copying is a violation of copyright law.

ISBN 978-1-56523-446-8

Library of Congress Cataloging-in-Publication Data

Rousseau, Rich.

Making wooden fishing lures / by Rich Rousseau
p. cm.

Includes index.

ISBN: 978-1-56523-446-8

1. Fishing lures. 2. Wood-carving. I. Title.

SH449.R68 2009
799.12'0284--dc22

2009040281

To learn more about the other great books from Fox Chapel Publishing, or to find a retailer near you, call toll-free 800-457-9112 or visit us at *www.FoxChapelPublishing.com*.

**Note to Authors:** We are always looking for talented authors to write new books. Please send a brief letter describing your idea to Acquisition Editor, 1970 Broad Street, East Petersburg, PA 17520.

Printed in Singapore
Tenth printing

# About the Author

Rich Rousseau has been carving wood for 49 years, and for 26 of those has been concentrating on fishing lures and decoys. He has been a dedicated fisherman since the age of 4 (nearly 60 years). He won the World Champion Fish Carving contest two years running, and has won numerous awards from Ducks Unlimited and Trout Unlimited for the amount of funds raised by the auction of his carvings for the organizations. The designs in this book are original— Rich says they "were thrown in the water, bitten, used, abused, and refined until they were perfected." He resides in northern Michigan, which is known for its lure making and fishing heritage.

## Acknowledgments

I would like to acknowledge the editorial staff and art department of Fox Chapel Publishing. Their help, tutoring, and patience made completing this book very easy, not to mention enjoyable.

# Foreword

One day last year, while on the water, I had one of those days. It was almost dark and I had not seen a fish all evening. As I started to make my last retrieve before heading in, I could see my newly made bait zigging and zagging through the water. I had only moved the bait a few feet when I saw a huge musky begin to approach. His head was as big as a pumpkin. His tail was as wide as a dinner plate. As I worked the bait closer to the boat, the fish got inches behind the bait. When the lure was just about to the boat, the water erupted as the musky thrashed, crushing the lure at boat side, and the battle was on.

I have always had a passion for fishing and for working with wood. Making my own wooden lures has enabled me to combine my interests. However, when finished, my lures looked square and bulky. Frankly, they sometimes acted more like a stick in the water than a baitfish. Other people on the water would watch me work my lures and ask if I had made it myself. I would respond by proudly acknowledging my skill with a bandsaw and a can of spray paint.

Rich helped me understand how some types of wood are too heavy to make good lures and how other types are too light. He helped me realize that without the right kind of wood, all of my time and work would be for nothing. He helped me find a pattern that would move more realistically through the water and that would effectively attract larger fish. Rich helped me understand how to place the weights correctly so the lure would literally swim through the water, acting exactly as a baitfish. Once I began incorporating Rich's suggestions into my carving and painting, my lures began to look sleek and professional. Every time I use them, someone is sure to approach and beg to know where I purchased them. Using the tips and patterns in this book will also help you make effective wooden lures. And I have to tell you, having people confuse your lure with something made professionally is way more gratifying than having people immediately know you made it yourself.

Have fun and enjoy.

**Paul Haarstad**

*Paul Haarstad has been fishing for 30 years. He works for Stamina Quality Components, one of the foremost lure parts supply businesses. The biggest musky caught on one of his handmade lures was 50 inches (1.3 meters) long and weighed 38 pounds (17 kilograms).*

# Table of Contents

# Introduction

Northern Michigan, where I'm from, has always been a hot bed of fishing lures. From Oscar Peterson to the Moonlight Bait Company, fishing is a long and honored tradition in this part of the country. I have always been fascinated with utilitarian objects that were also considered an art form. What is it, exactly, that made some of these objects classics? The one thing in common with all of the classic lures is their simplicity. The most desirable ones all seem to have been reduced to their bare essentials, and executed well.

That's where this book comes in. Chapter 1 covers the basics: everything you need to know about wood, types of lures, and more is located there. Chapter 3 explains some extra options you have when creating your very own lures—you can make a jointed lure, a super-strong wired lure, or even dress your own hooks. The appendix houses 15 bonus lure patterns to help develop your skills even further. The gallery of antique and modern lures in the front of the book is there to serve as inspiration. Fishy facts—fun and interesting fishing tips—are spread throughout the book on the page bottoms. Keep your eyes open for other entertaining stories and tidbits featured in boxes here and there! However, the bulk of the book consists of the 11 step-by-step lure projects in Chapter 2. Each project includes a detailed pattern and pages of step-by-step photos to guide your construction.

# Lure-making basics—It's easy, cheap, and fun!

Making a lure is easy, affordable, and fun. The four steps you see below are the basics needed to make any lure. Plenty of detail is shown in the step-by-step projects, but as long as you hit these four steps, you'll have a lure that works.

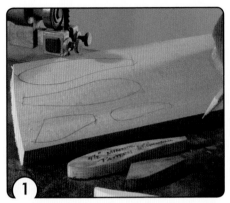

**Shape the lure body.** You'll start with a purchased lure rough-out, a dowel rod, or some scrap wood.

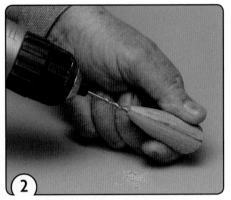

**Drill the pilot holes.** Every lure has hardware (a.k.a. hooks, eye screws, counter weights, etc.), and hardware requires pilot holes to keep the lure from splitting in half.

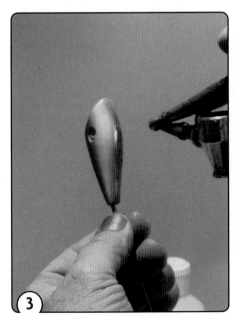

**Paint the lure.** There are three ways demonstrated in this book to paint your lure—acrylic and brushes, spray paint, and airbrush.

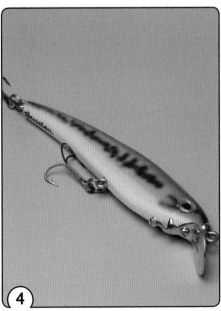

**Apply finishing touches.** Put in the eyes, sign your name, put on the clear coat, and attach that hardware! That's all it takes.

# Lure Gallery

Lure collecting is a hobby that will keep you thinking fishing all year long, no matter what the weather is.

One area of interest is homemade or handcrafted: call them what you want, but they are usually one-of-a-kind lures. They are the creation of someone who was dreaming of a lure that would entice the "Big One" and then made it. The color schemes, sizes, and shapes are as different as the people who make them. Some have great action in the water and are actually made with using them in mind.

When searching for lures, the homemade style is always on my mind. When I find one, I ask what it is—at times I hear, "Oh, it's just an old homemade lure." My next question is, "What will you take for it?" I appreciate the time and effort it took to make that lure, and I'm now sharing the fishing dream of its maker. Like I said before, call them what you want, I call them folk art and I love them. So you keep on making them and people like me will keep on seeking them to hang on our den walls to share your dream.

Happy carving and collecting!

**Butch Bartz**

Heddon. Pumpkinseed. circa 1940.

Heddon. Dowagiac #100 minnow. Early 1900s.

*Over the past 26 years, Butch Bartz has amassed more than 5,000 lures in his collection. A few of the better-known makers he has collected include: commercial makers Creek-Chub, Paw Paw, Heddons, Winneys,' and Shakespeare; and individual carvers Ron and Don Hosney of Livonia, Mich., Bud Stewart of Alpena, Mich., Oscar Peterson of Kalkaska, Mich., Burt and Art Winney of Traverse City, Mich., and Carl Christiansen of Mich.*

*Unless otherwise noted, the lures shown in this gallery are all from Butch's collection.*

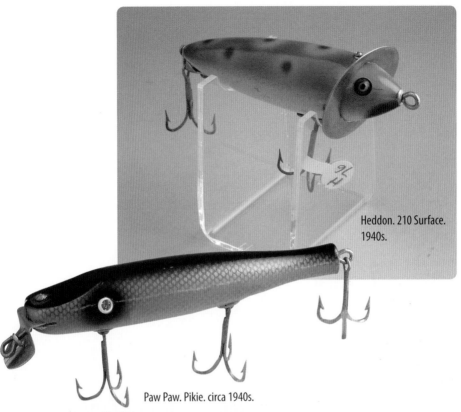

Heddon. 210 Surface. 1940s.

Paw Paw. Pikie. circa 1940s.

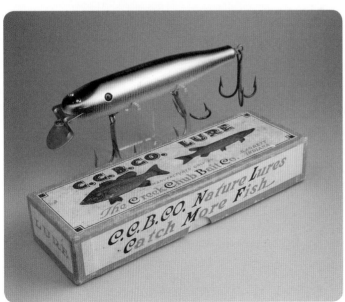

Creek Chub. Pikie. 1940 to 1950.

Paw Paw.
Weedless Wow.
1940s.

Shakespeare. Slim Jim (6541 YP).
1924 to 1950.

BAITS THAT CATCH FISH

*Shakespeare*

HONOR BUILT FOR OVER FIFTY YEARS

Shakespeare Company
FINE FISHING TACKLE
*Kalamazoo U.S.A.*

GOOD FISHING

BEGINS HERE

Paw Paw. Wotta-Frog. 1941 to 1960.

Ron Hosney, Kalkaska, Mich. Brown Mouse 8, fly-rod lure. Post-1980.

Unknown Michigan maker, Alger Area, Mich., circa post-1980.

Elman "Bud" Stewart, Alpena, Mich., area, now deceased. Post-1980.

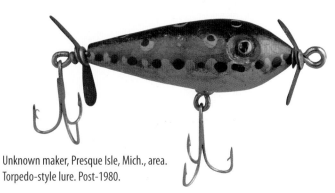

Unknown maker, Presque Isle, Mich., area. Torpedo-style lure. Post-1980.

fishy fact

Fish for pike at the mouths of streams or rivers.

Gerald Finch, Cheboygan, Mich., area. Beaver musky lure. Post-1980.

Gerald Finch, Cheboygan, Mich., area. Rainbow musky lure. Post-1980.

Unknown Michigan maker.

Unknown maker, Upper Peninsula, Mich., area. Circa post-1980.

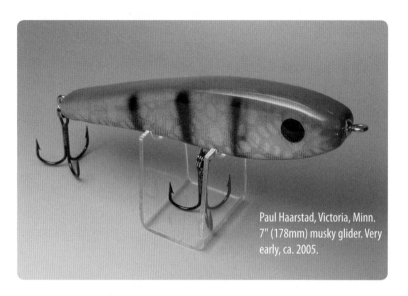

Paul Haarstad, Victoria, Minn. 7" (178mm) musky glider. Very early, ca. 2005.

Unknown maker, Alpena, Mich., area. Flat fish type. Circa post-1980.

Rich Rousseau. In-shore saltwater, 6" (152mm) floater/ diver. Designed for a friend in Florida, but used in Michigan as a musky bait. 2007. (From Rich's tackle box.)

Paul Haarstad, Victoria, Minn. 7" (178mm) musky glider. 2009.

## Tackle box addition

Another handy little item to keep in your tackle box is one of those multi-tool gizmos. They are worth their weight in gold for dealing with those unexpected problems—anything from repairing a reel to cutting a hook out of your hand.

Rich Rousseau. 6" (152mm) sinking baby pike. Designed for Northern pike and musky. 2000. (From Rich's tackle box.)

Rich Rousseau. 3¼" (83mm) bass lure, floater/diver. 1998. (From Rich's tackle box.)

Rich Rousseau. 1¾" (44mm) blue-gill and crappie floater/diver. 1997. (From Rich's tackle box.)

## The most important thing

The absolute most important item in any fishing arsenal is a well-made beverage holder—so important, in fact, that you should spare no expense in acquiring a good one.

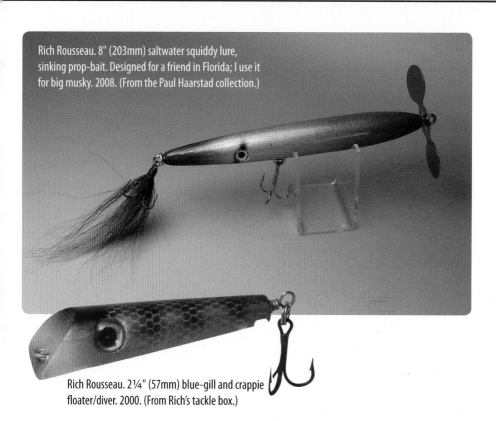

Rich Rousseau. 8" (203mm) saltwater squiddy lure, sinking prop-bait. Designed for a friend in Florida; I use it for big musky. 2008. (From the Paul Haarstad collection.)

Rich Rousseau. 2¼" (57mm) blue-gill and crappie floater/diver. 2000. (From Rich's tackle box.)

Rich Rousseau. 3" (76mm) bass lure, sinking and wiggling, experimental. 2000. (From Rich's tackle box.)

Rich Rousseau. 4½" (114mm) bass bait surface/prop. 2009. (From Rich's tackle box.)

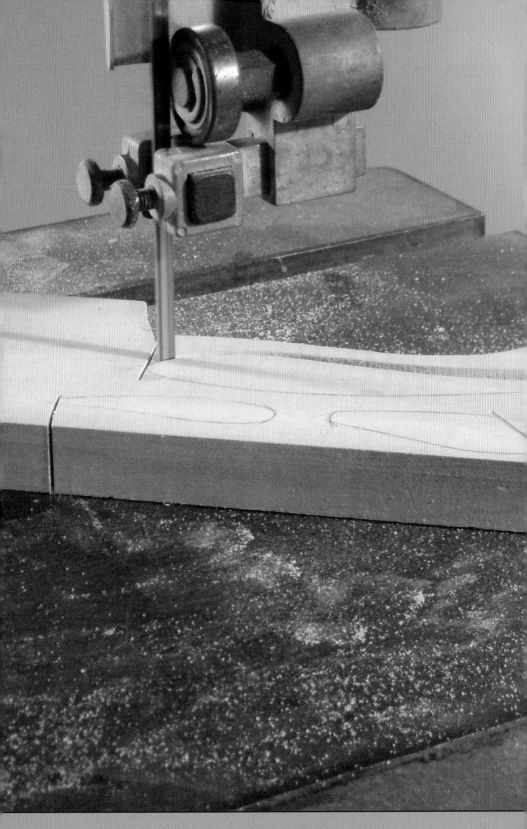

# CHAPTER 1

# Getting Started

Making wooden lures is easy—you don't need a shop full of tools, a barn full of paint, or a Ph.D. in science to create a fine fishing lure. Heck, you don't even have to mortgage the house for material purchases! This section will show you what you need to create the wooden lures in this book. Tools, hardware—it's all here! You'll also learn about the different types of lures and how they work.

# Lure Types

Lures are categorized by the action they perform while in the water and being retrieved (when you reel them back in). There are four general types of lures: surface, floating-diving, sinking, and keel-weighted. Let's take a look at precisely what these lures do and why.

## Surface lures

A surface lure floats and continues to float as it is retrieved. A **popper** has a cupped flat face and splashes water as it is retrieved in short, sharp jerks. A **jitterbug** has an angled flat face that produces a rhythmic "plop-plop" as it is retrieved steadily. A **surface prop bait** has propellers that slap the water. And heck, there's even a lure that has arms sticking out on the sides that grab water and wiggle the lure back and forth—that's a **crawler**.

A surface lure attracts fish by making noise and surface disturbance that fish sense from a long distance. Surface lures are effective regardless of water depth and can be used in both shallow areas as well as the middle of the lake.

## Floating-diving lures

Floating-diving lures float while at rest and dive below the surface when retrieved. This type can have a diving lip or a cupped and angled face. The angle of the diving plane determines the depth to which the lure will descend. If the plane of the lip is nearly parallel to the lure, it will dive very deep; as the lip approaches 90° to the body, it will not dive as deeply. Keep in mind that the speed of the retrieve will affect depth as well—the faster the retrieve, the deeper the dive. Nearly all floating-diving lures wiggle back-and-forth when retrieved because the flat face is unstable when pulled through the water. The wiggle attracts fish by both creating a sound-pulse or pressure wave and making the color pattern flash. If you crank it back fast, it will wiggle fast; if you retrieve it slowly, it will wiggle slowly. Normally these lures will run from about 2 feet (610mm) deep to about 20 feet (6,096mm) deep.

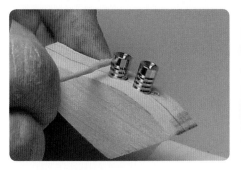
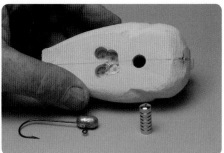

## Sinking lures

As the name implies, sinking lures are heavier than water and sink. This type of lure includes some wooden lures, as well as metal spinners and spoons. Just because they sink, don't think these lures can't wiggle, produce sound and flash, and include propellers, spinner blades and the like. These lures are effective when the fish are feeding at depth. Most sinking lures have a sink-rate of about 1 foot (305mm) per second and can, therefore, be counted down. When the lure hits the water, start counting "thousand and one," "thousand and two," etc. and before you start your retrieve, you will have a fair idea of how deep the lure is running. You can even let the lure sink to the bottom before retrieving it, which is effective for any bottom-hugging predator species, such as freshwater walleye.

Note that propellers and spinner blades generate lift. This fact can help you design certain features into the lure, as well as allow you some creative retrieve patterns—i.e., retrieve quickly (the lure rises), then slow down or pause (the lure will sink).

## Keel-weighted lures

If you wish to make a lure that will resemble a real bait fish, realize that a flat board will not float on its edge. You need to add weights inside the belly to make it float (or sink) belly down. In the case of a cupped-face floater-diver, you may wish to keel weight the very front to ensure that the cupped face will dig into the water and start working immediately. Where you place the keel weights is important because they affect the action of the lure. Basically, if the keel weight is toward the rear of the lure, the action slows down. This means that if you made a lure that wiggles way too fast, you can add a small keel weight toward the rear end, and the lure's action will slow down. The keel weights also affect the attitude of the lure in the water, i.e., you can make a lure run head-down or head-up or neutral simply by where you place the weights. A secondary use for the keel weight is in a lure you wish to retrieve very quickly—the keel weight will not allow the lure to turn over. In other words, it will remain belly down no matter how fast you bring it back.

**Dispose of waste properly when fishing—take it home with you.**

# Modifying lures for species

There is no such thing as a fish-specific lure. Generally, you try to use a lure of a certain size, color, and action to entice the species you are trying to catch. However, I have caught blue-gills on bass baits, and large Northern pike on tiny trout baits. I have even had large pike attack other fish I've already hooked. Basically, color pattern and size are what determines the species, not the lure type. By selecting the correct size, any type of lure can be effective on *all* species. Nobody knows for sure what a fish wants on any given day—that's why there are so many types, sizes, and colors of lures. My advice is start with a lure you think might be right and keep changing lures until the fish tell you what they want! Otherwise, you may wind up scratching your head and imbibing a wee bit too much of your favorite beverage.

## Size

As a general rule of thumb, most anglers choose lures for size, color, and other considerations based upon the size and disposition of the fish they wish to catch. As you look over this information, realize it is a guideline only. I want to give you a starting point when you choose to build a lure for a specific type of fish, but as with everything, there are always exceptions to any so-called rule. The chart at right shows you approximate measurements for the lure body by species and extra hardware. For example, if you want to make a plain-old smallmouth bass lure, you should create or select a lure body between 1 to 3" (25 to 76mm)-long. If you want a smallmouth bass lure with a chaser, keep the body between 1 and 2" (25 to 51mm).

A good way to judge your lure size selection is to observe how the fish took the lure. If a fish has swallowed the entire lure and you are having a lot of trouble getting it out of his face, you may want to get a bigger lure or at the very least, bigger hooks. Likewise, if fish are hitting your lure but not becoming hooked, you may wish to reduce the size of the lure or the hooks.

## Color

Color patterns are mostly regional. While there are general guidelines, each region has peculiarities unique to the area and water. I know that sounds like a cop out, but it is true. Generally, colors such as gold, silver, red, and orange are good places to start. You will usually have to add some regional pattern—surprisingly, "mindless" predators can be pretty picky. Generally speaking, colors should be relative to the bait in any given body of water. Use that as a starting point and add bells and whistles from there.

# Lure size chart

| Species | Size of lure body | Size of lure to add dressed rear hook | Size of lure to add front chaser | Size of lure to add propeller(s) |
|---|---|---|---|---|
| Bluegills, sunfish, perch, crappie, trout less than 12" (305mm) | 1–2" (25–51mm) | 1–1½" (25–38mm) | 1" (25mm) | 1–2" (25–51mm) |
| Smallmouth bass | 1–3" (25–76mm) | 1–2" (25–51mm) | 1–2" (25–51mm) | 1–3" (25–76mm) |
| Largemouth bass | 2–4" (51–102mm) | 2–3½" (51–89mm) | 2–3" (51–76mm) | 2–4" (51–102mm) |
| Walleye, large-size bass | 2–5" (51–127mm) | 2–4" (51–102mm) | 2–3½" (51–89mm) | 2–5" (51–127mm) |
| Northern pike, less than 30" (762mm) | 2½–4" (64–102mm) | 2½–3" (64–76mm) | 2½–3½" (64–89mm) | 2½–4" (64–102mm) |
| Northern pike, larger than 30" (762mm) | 3½–6½" (89–165mm) | 3½–5" (89–127mm) | 3½–5" (89–127mm) | 3½–6½" (89–165mm) |
| Trout and salmon, 12–24" (305–610mm) | 2–4" (51–102mm) | 2–3" (51–76mm) | 2–3½" (51–89mm) | 2–4" (51–102mm) |
| Trout and salmon, larger than 24" (610mm) | 3–5" (76–127mm) | 3–4½" (76–114mm) | 3–4¼" (76–108mm) | 3–5" (76–127mm) |
| Muskellunge, larger than 40" (102mm) | 5–12" (127–305mm) | 5–11½" (127–292mm) | 5–10" (127–254mm) | 5–11½" (127–292mm) |

## Fly rod baits

The size of fly rod lures are a matter of weight and air resistance. The lure must fall within certain weight restrictions if it is going to actually be cast. As with regular flies, you may have to rely on sinking tips, or the like, if you need the lure to submerge. Normally you will need to keep a wooden fly rod lure to 3" (76mm) maximum; 1 to 2" (25 to 51mm) is best.

## Saltwater lures

My experience with saltwater fishing had a steep learning curve. There are so many variables that a hard and fast rule does not exist. I would highly recommend that when you make a lure you should know the favorite size of lure commonly used by local anglers. The same would apply to color preferences.

"Nothing makes a fish bigger than almost being caught."

# Wood

There are several types of wood that make better lures than others due to their density, workability, and a few other factors. My favorite types include SPF construction lumber, dowel rods, and pre-shaped lure bodies. Wood choice is simply a matter of practicality. A majority of saltwater game fish have cutting jaws or really hard pointed teeth and other anatomical features that are very hard on lure bodies. Dense wood is the best choice for saltwater lures because it resists damage better. For example, a spruce or poplar dowel is half the weight and about one-third to one-half the density of a mahogany dowel.

Freshwater game fish and the appropriate fishing tackle is not nearly as heavy as saltwater fish and tackle, so use heavier weight woods for saltwater and medium weight woods for freshwater. For the purposes of fishing lures, equate the weight of wood with its density. If it is heavy, then it is also dense. Use the heavy wood for the tough fish and the medium wood for freshwater fish (except Northern pike and muskies).

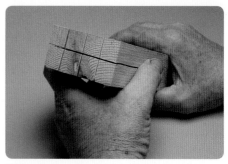

SPF lumber is a cheap source of lure material.

## SPF construction lumber

For most of my lures, I use spruce, pine, and fir (SPF) construction lumber. Those three woods are medium density, meaning they are easily worked and finished, accept paint well, and are durable. The woods are not too heavy, so they don't hurt the rod or wrist. They also are not too light, so they cast into the wind and float consistently well, and fish can't chew them up in just a few bites. SPF lumber can be found as 2 by 4s up to 2 by 10s or even 1 by 2s. You can obtain this wood from construction sites, roof truss plants, and large lumber stores.

All three species are excellent for lures, but there are minor differences you should be aware of. You can easily differentiate spruce from pine and fir, because it is noticeably lighter in weight and usually lighter in color. The pine will have less prominent grain showing than will the fir, but this is not always the case. For the purposes of making lures, pine and fir are considered the same.

Dowels are a great source for lure wood.

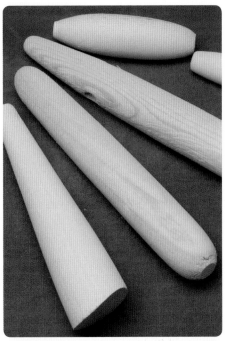

# Dowel rods

Dowel rods are a useful second option for lure wood, because part of the shaping has already been done for you. You can purchase them, quite cheaply, from any large chain store, craft store, lumberyard, or hardware store. Most available dowels are poplar, which is fairly grainless, the right density, and durable. If you pick out the lightest dowel in the bunch, it will be the easiest to work into a lure suitable for most game fish. Conversely, if you are making lures for saltwater species, Northern pike, or muskellunge, you want denser, harder wood—simply pick out one of the heavier dowels. A $3 dowel of 36" (914mm) length will make eleven 3" (76mm) lures; that's about 28 cents per lure, which is not exactly expensive.

## Pre-shaped lure bodies

The third source of wood is to buy rough-shaped wooden lure bodies from a tackle supplier. These need only be sanded, and you're ready to go. They cost from $1.98 up to $3.98 for the bigger sizes. This costs more than getting your wood for free, but it is also a lot less work. Since the whole idea is to have some fun making lures, I leave it to you which way you would like to go. I'm going to show you how to do it from scratch; however, it's always good to know your options.

# Tools

Now that we have the wood thing covered, let's move on to tools. Some of the tools listed will make your work easier, but are by no means necessary, and I will clearly tell you which is which.

Keep in mind that I only have the complete use of one hand so I have to do a lot of improvising. Please consider that fact as you read my use of tools and decide for yourself if that use is appropriate for you.

## Band saw

A band saw is very useful, but not mandatory. A band saw allows for precise cuts, cutting down large pieces into small lure bodies, and tapering cuts. You have the advantage of holding the wood with both hands and letting the tool do the work. This does not mean a band saw is the only way to get the job done—just the easiest. Generally, a coping saw or scroll saw is too light-duty to cut out lure bodies from medium density wood between ¾" and 2" (19mm and 51mm) thick.

Since you will be cutting small pieces, even a small saw will be a great help. The size of a band saw is measured from the blade to the side of the upright support arm. A 14" (356mm) band saw is great, but so is a 6 to 8" (152 to 203mm). The smaller saws are inexpensive because they are not as useful to furniture makers and the like.

The photos in this book show a raised guard on my band saw; this was done for photographic clarity. However, make sure

A band saw is very useful for lure making, but not essential.

that your blade guard is in the proper position—be safe!

## Belt sander

A belt sander is a useful, but not mandatory, tool. This tool makes rough shaping easier, as well as tapering dowel rods or making square stock into round stock. It also makes it easy to angle the lure heads, if needed. Even a handheld belt sander may be clamped into a vise by its handle and used in place of a bench model. Having said that, you may also whittle the body to rough shape, hand sand with a sanding block you make yourself, and get equally good results.

A belt sander will come in handy for rough shaping.

# Sanding blocks

You can purchase sanding blocks, but generally I prefer to make them myself. You can glue sandpaper to any shape of wood (block, dowel, ball, etc.) and have a shaping tool designed to do any job you wish. Apply the same idea to a flat stationary sander made by gluing sandpaper to a flat, heavy piece of sheet steel scrap obtained from the local welding shop.

The only exception to the sanding block rule is that I do buy emery boards because they cost less than making them. I like the foam boards; these come in all types of grit from fine to coarse and they are cheap. You can get these at any of the big chain stores. Even grocery stores carry them. I use the coarse grit for light shaping and the fine grit for sealer coats and between paint coats.

These are some examples of sanding blocks that you make yourself.

This is my utility knife, an old model bought at a yard sale for 75 cents.

# Knives

I favor a utility knife for my carving blade because you can spend your time carving and not sharpening the blade. If you choose to use a utility knife, make sure it is the type that locks the blade down tightly and not the type where the blade slides in and out with a thumb latch. When the blade gets the least bit dull, flip it over to the other end. When that edge gets dull, throw the blade away and put in a new one. You are carving—not sharpening.

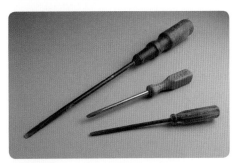

Here is my set of dedicated lure-making screwdrivers.

# Screwdrivers

Most of the hardware used in making lures is fairly small. I use screwdrivers with small blades and relatively long shanks. I bought mine from yard sales for less than a dollar, and then shaped the blades with a file to suit my needs.

## Punches and pin-pricks

Punches and pin-pricks are handy and simple to make yourself. Basically, you want a needle with a handle. You can make these by shortening an old-fashioned hat-pin or reshaping a dental tool. I get my dental picks from dentists for free because they often have some that are bent or broken. You can also get dental picks from discount tool supply catalogs.

To make a punch from scratch, find an old-fashioned hat-pin with a big round head, shorten the pin to about 1" (25mm), and file it sharp again. You can also glue a large needle into a wooden handle; grab a scrap piece of wood, some five-minute epoxy, and you are all set. These items are especially good for making pilot holes for small screws, lifting 3-D eyes, and a lot of other small jobs.

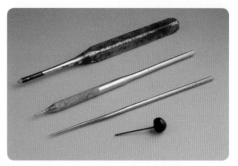

These are some of the types of pin punches that I make.

## Pliers and cutters

I use specialized pliers for tackle making. First you will want a pair of small bent needle-nose pliers. You will also find it handy to have the following types of pliers: regular needle-nose, round-end (wire-forming), and split-ring pliers. You will also find that a pair of side cutters, also known as dikes, is almost indispensable.

These tools are available from tackle supply houses (see Resources), craft shops and suppliers, or big chain stores. Don't overlook that great American supply house—the yard sale—either.

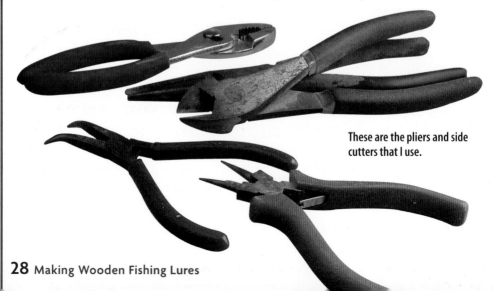

These are the pliers and side cutters that I use.

## Drill bits

You can use any type of drill bits for lure making, but there are some jobs where a couple of certain drill bits will make your job easier and the overall results better. When drilling eye holes, keel-weight holes, or holes to set washers, you cannot beat brad-point and Forstner bits. These bits drill precise holes with flat bottoms. A counter-sink bit comes in handy as well.

I have been making these lures for years upon years, and so am very comfortable holding the lures in one hand while drilling with the other hand. However, this may not be the safest method for you. Be aware that holding the lure in your hand can result in the lure spinning and giving you a nasty whack on the knuckles, not to mention the possibility of an errant drill bit going who-knows-where. If you're unsure, be safe and secure your lure in a bench vise. Sandwich the lure between pieces of scrap wood to prevent marring.

## Scale netting

To paint scales on your lures, you can purchase professional nylon netting or you can make your own. I use the soft scrubbies found at the grocery store. The type sold as pot scrubbers have finer weave than the ones sold as bathing aids. Use the pot scrubbers on the smaller lures and the people scrubbers on the larger lures. Separate them in the middle by untying or removing the staple,

I use two types of scrubbers to paint scale netting—pot (left) and people (right).

Here is the type of clothespins that I use. Notice that the pin in the foreground shows the modifications we talked about.

and they'll fold out into a large strip of netting, ready to be cut to size.

## Clothespins

You will find it very handy to have a supply of clothespins on hand. They are useful as small clamps. Common clothespins are inexpensive and available almost everywhere. They need to be modified just slightly, however. I cut the V on the clamp end off flat, and then sand it smooth. This modification allows for a very tight fitting of the scale netting to the lure.

Fish like to lurk near objects in the water—dock pilings, weeds, etc.

Acrylic paints, applied with brushes, are one way to paint your lures.

## Painting tools

There are basically three ways to paint your lures. First, you can paint them with artist's brushes and acrylic (or the like). Second, you can paint your lures with common spray paint—the kind that comes in aerosol cans. Finally, you can paint them with an airbrush and the paint of your choice. We will examine all three methods in our first three projects, but you can see in the three photographs the actual types of equipment I use to make my lures.

You can use normal spray paint to decorate your lures.

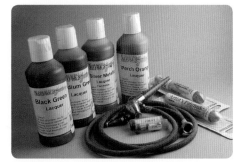

An airbrush is a third way to paint lures.

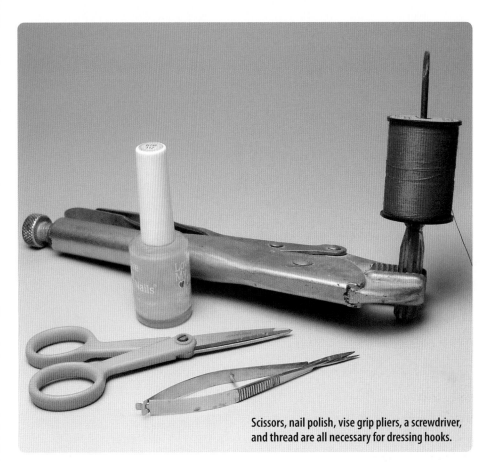

Scissors, nail polish, vise grip pliers, a screwdriver, and thread are all necessary for dressing hooks.

# Hook-dressing tools

A few other tools that come in handy for dressing hooks include scissors, clear nail polish for sealing the knot, and a setup with a vise grip pliers and a screwdriver to hold the thread spool. A clamp to hold the hook while dressing makes the operation much safer.

The last word on tools is to be really careful—not of using the tools, but rather that these little buggers will sneak up on you. You will be at a yard sale, minding your own business, and a little voice will speak up: "Take me home, take me home!" The next thing you know, your tool bench is out of control. Be careful, 'cause lure tools are very sneaky.

## No-snag lure drying

Keep a paper towel in your fishing gear. You can dry your lures before putting them away, and the hooks can't snag the wipe. If they do, the paper will simply tear away from the hook.

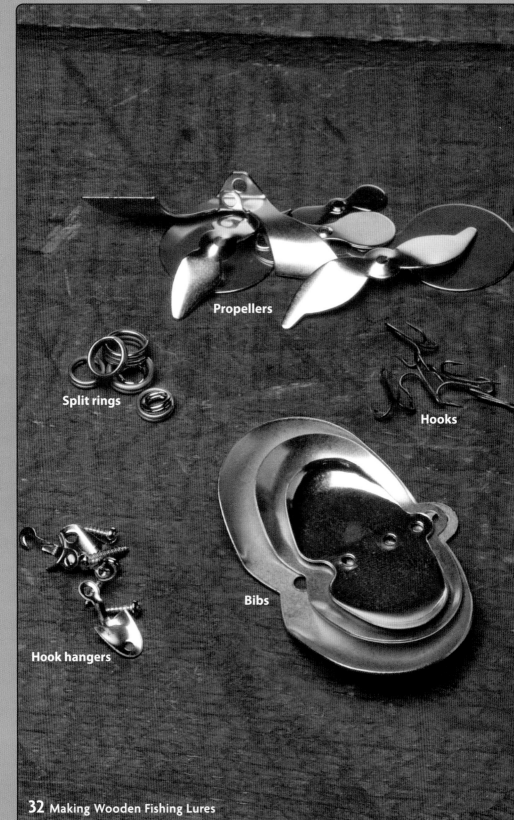

**Propellers**

**Split rings**

**Hooks**

**Hook hangers**

**Bibs**

# Hardware

The little parts that go into and onto fishing lures represent one area that can really get under your skin. The problem is that there are literally thousands of different lure accoutrements, and every one of them will look useful to you. There are eye screws, regular screws, and split rings, lots of washers, beads, propellers, blades, clevises, and on and on. The other problem is that the parts are not very expensive, so the next thing you know you will have bins full of small parts, and won't remember what the heck you got them for.

A good way to approach hardware is to decide what types of lures you really like, check over the how-to photographs, and decide what hardware you like the look or function of. Then, look through a parts catalogue (or online store) to determine what sizes of, and how many parts, you actually need. After your initial few lures, you will have a good handle on what purchases to make. A good example is the stainless-steel wire I use in making lures. You can buy various wires from the parts catalogue for very little money, and that is what I used to do myself. Now I use stainless steel wire that the fellas at the welding shop give to me for free. The lesson here is use whatever you like.

**Propellers:** Propellers are used to add flash and movement to a lure as it is being retrieved. There are many sizes and shapes of propeller.

**Hooks:** Treble hooks have three barbs and come in a range of sizes. The sizes I most commonly use for freshwater lures are 8, 6, 4, and 2. The bigger the number, the smaller the hook. On most lures, hooks can be found on the belly and in the rear. The rear hook is usually the same size as the belly hook or one to two sizes larger, depending upon the desire of the maker. As long as they do not interfere with each other the hook size is irrelevant.

**Split rings:** Split rings are used to attach a hook or other movable piece of hardware to an eye screw.

**Bibs:** Bibs are attached to the front of surface lures to make them skip across the water when being retrieved. This skipping action will also make a "plop, plop, plop" noise that attracts some fish. There are three sizes (small, medium, large). Bib sizes are usually chosen to match the overall size of the lure. You can put small bibs on large lures for subtle noise and action, but a large bib will make a small lure sink.

**Hook hangers:** Hook hangers are used to secure a hook directly to the lure body. Hangers need hanger screws to attach the hardware to the lure. The small hanger gets ¼" (6mm)-long screws and the medium hangers get ⅜" (10mm).

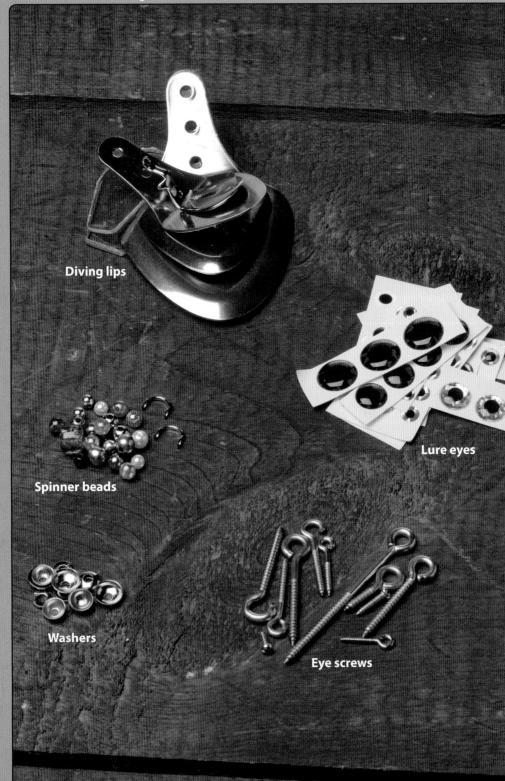

**Diving lips**

**Lure eyes**

**Spinner beads**

**Washers**

**Eye screws**

**Diving lips:** Diving lips are attached to the front of a diving lure so that, when retrieved, it will dive. Diving lips are available in a variety of sizes and shapes—once again, choice is up to the lure maker. See Floating-diving lures, page 20.

**Lure eyes:** Lure eyes come in a variety of colors and sizes. They can be two-dimensional or three-dimensional.

**Eye screws:** Eye screws are used to attach other hardware or hooks to the lure and also to serve as a line-tie. Open eye screws have a small gap in the ring that allows the insertion of a split ring or hook. Closed eye screws do not have that gap. Eye screws are very similar and range from ½ to 2" (13mm to 51mm) in length and have three diameters: .050", .072", and .092". Basically, you pick the size you want that will fit on the lure. Obviously, you cannot put 2" (51mm) screws in both ends of a 3" (76mm) lure.

**Washers:** Washers come in two types: flat and cupped. Cup washers are used as bearings so that propellers spin freely. They are also used to limit hook swing, so the hook points will not damage the lure body or foul up another hook. Flat washers are used as a wear-guard when hooks swing on an eye screw, and are also used as a finish piece on high-end lures to improve aesthetics. Both washer types come in two sizes—¼" or 5⁄16" (6mm or 8mm). Select washers based on the size of the hook and screw.

Hey, enough of this boring stuff. Let's get to the projects and have some fun. Grab a beverage and a comfy chair and let's housebreak this puppy.

## Fish on film

Keep a disposable camera in your tackle box for those "trophies" that you want to release. When it's full and been processed, the memories are priceless.

# CHAPTER 2

# Lure Step-by-Step Projects

Get ready for 11 lure projects you can make in a jiffy. No matter what type of fish you're trying to catch, you'll find a lure here to catch it. Dive right in!

# Surface Prop Bait

Our first project is going to be a pure classic bass lure: a surface prop bait. We are going to make this lure from **scrap 2 by 4** and **paint it by hand** with brushes and acrylic paint. Hand-painted lures have a look all their own, and you may be surprised at how nice the overall results are. I hope you enjoy this project.

# Surface Prop Bait Pattern

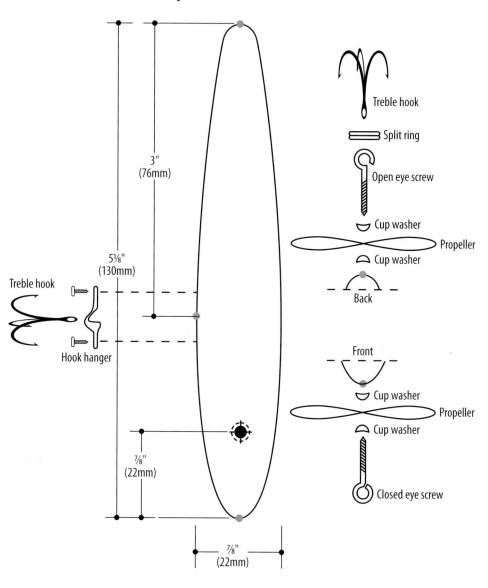

Treble hook

Split ring

Open eye screw

Cup washer

Propeller

Cup washer

Back

3"
(76mm)

5⅛"
(130mm)

Treble hook

Hook hanger

Front

Cup washer

Propeller

Cup washer

Closed eye screw

⅞"
(22mm)

⅞"
(22mm)

**Photocopy at 100%**

# Materials and tools list

## Materials
- Scrap 2 by 4
- 2" (51mm) eye screw (handle)
- Lure eyes
- Toothpick
- Five-minute epoxy

## Hardware
### Bottom assembly:
- Hook hanger and screws
- Treble hook

### Front assembly:
- Closed eye screw
- 2 cup washers
- Propeller

### Rear assembly:
- Open eye screw
- Split ring
- 2 cup washers
- Propeller
- Treble hook

## Tools
- Band saw or handsaw
- Heavy flat sander
- Vise
- Soft lead pencil
- Foam-core emery board
- Flexible ruler
- Handheld power drill
- Countersink bit
- 5/16" (8mm) brad-point bit
- Prick punch
- 1/32" (1mm) drill bit

- Rag and acetone
- Small scale netting from pot scrubber
- Modified clothespins
- Paper towels
- Fine point permanent ink pen
- Needle-nose pliers
- Split-ring pliers

## Painting supplies
- Flat white spray paint
- Acrylic paints: red, neon orange, leaf green, metallic gold, black, and tan
- Hair dryer
- Small brush
- Stippling brush
- Small pointed brush
- Size 0 script liner brush
- Clear spray finish

### Shape the body

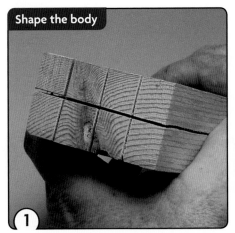

**1** Use a band saw or handsaw to cut your 2 by 4 as shown. Note that these 4 cuts do not go all the way through. Make sure the cuts are longer than the lure you wish to make. Cut the board off to the correct length and you have your 8 lure body blanks.

**2** Use your heavy flat sander (or your flat hand sander locked in a vise) to sand the square body into the shape of an octagon.

3 This is what your octagon should look like after this stage. The octagon does not have to be exact, just close to having the sides even.

4 When you are satisfied with your 8 sides, repeat the process with the new corners so that you produce a 16-sided stick. You can see that the original square is now almost round.

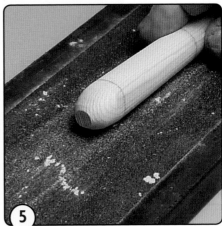

5 Notice the two pencil lines in this shot. There is one near the head and one near the tail. These lines are guides for rounding off the head and tapering the tail.

6 Taper the tail so it is sanded and nearly round.

fishy fact

**Each species of fish has a certain temperature range it prefers.**

41

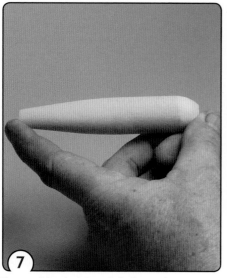

**7** Your rough lure body is ready for fine sanding.

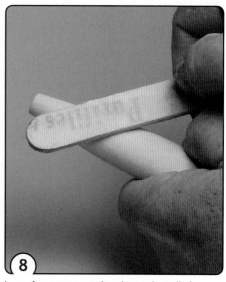

**8** I use a foam-core emery board to sand out all of the heavy tool marks. You do not have to have a mirror-smooth finish; just eliminate any obvious cuts, scratches, dents, and the like.

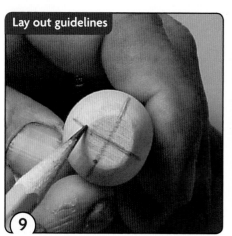

**Lay out guidelines**

**9** It is now time to get some centerlines on this guy. Start by drawing a North/South line on the nose and an East/West line (90° to the first line) to form a cross. The ends of these lines should go back onto the sides of the lure about 1/16" (2mm). Look at the lure nose-on and it will be easy to see if you have even quadrants.

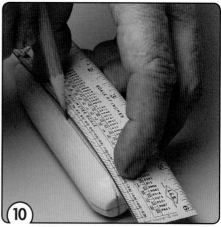

**10** Pick one of the lines to become the center of the back, and no, it doesn't matter which one. Grab your small flexible ruler and draw a line down the middle of the back. Make a second cross on the tail end of the lure and draw in your ventral (or belly) centerline as well.

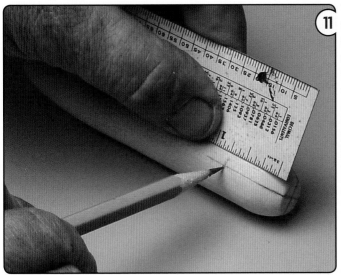

**11** The two sides of the cross that are not centerlines will help you find your eye lines. Draw along your flexible ruler to about 1½" (38mm) from the nose. Find wherever you want to have the center of your lure eyes and make a mark that crosses the eye line. X marks the spot, as it were.

## Checking symmetry

By looking at the nose and tail end of the lure alternately, it will be readily apparent if your two centerlines do not line up symmetrically.

## Avoid embossing

Always use a soft lead pencil and a very light touch when drawing centerlines; that way you will not emboss a groove in the wood.

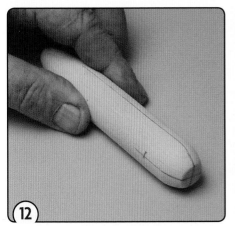

**12** After drawing on all of your lines, look over the lure carefully. Look at the front and back, top and bottom, and all around, checking for symmetry. Make any necessary corrections. It is now time to start laying out your hardware.

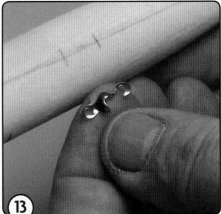

**13** Since our lure will have a hook hanger on the belly, let's start with that. Take the actual hanger and place it on the belly centerline in the correct location. Mark the center of the two screw holes onto the centerline.

fishy fact

Most fish move toward the shore when water rises.

**Drill pilot holes**

**14** Your next step is use a countersink bit to drill a cup at the nose and tail, right in the center of your crosses. The reason for the chamfering is that the pilot hole drill bit is so small (about ⅟₃₂" [1mm]), the wood grain will make it wander off center very easily if you do not.

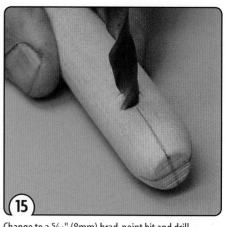

**15** Change to a ⁵⁄₁₆" (8mm) brad-point bit and drill the eyeholes. Remember to secure the lure in a bench vise if you don't feel comfortable holding it by hand.

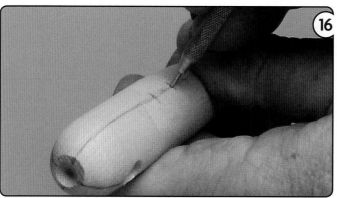

**16** Roll the lure over to its belly side and use your prick punch to make your two hook hanger screw holes. These screws are too small to use a pilot hole bit—besides, this is more accurate and faster to boot.

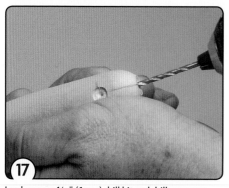

**17** Load up your ⅟₃₂" (1mm) drill bit and drill your nose and tail pilot holes. The chamfers that you cut with the countersink bit will make this easier and more accurate.

## Crooked pilot holes?

If any of your pilot holes are drilled off-center or in the wrong place, it's an easy fix. Dip a wooden toothpick in some glue and drive it into the hole. Either cut or break it off and sand it smooth. It will be good as new and like they say, "No harm, no foul."

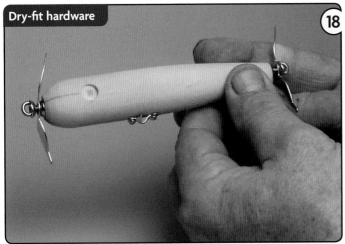

**Dry-fit hardware**

**18** We are now going to dry fit all of the hardware. It is not necessary to run all the screws down tight. Just run them in and stop a little short of seating them. This step prevents damaging your finished lure—there will not be any stubborn screws to cause a screwdriver slip or such.

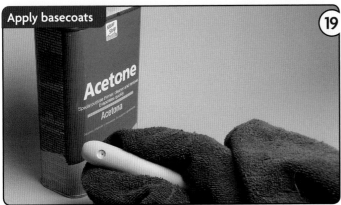

**Apply basecoats**

**19** Remove all of the hardware and set it aside (a sandwich baggy works well for this procedure). Because of all of the handling and sanding, you will want to degrease the lure body. Dampen a rag with acetone and thoroughly wipe it down. Don't soak the rag—just dampen it.

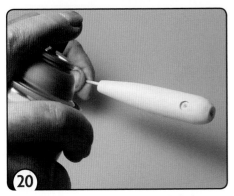

**20** Install a handle so you won't have to touch the lure body directly while painting. Use an eye screw about 2" (51mm) long and the same diameter as your finished screw. Spray the lure body with flat white paint (see tips, right).

## Spray painting

Wear disposable gloves while painting to avoid technicolored hands. When spray painting, spray from 12" (305mm) away and use at least two or three light coats. These light coats will dry faster and more completely than will one heavy coat. Hang the lure and let it dry 12 to 18 hours. If you do not let the basecoat dry thoroughly, the scale netting will actually emboss into the uncured paint or lift it right off the lure.

fishy fact

Most fish can spot blue and purple lures in deep water.

We are now ready to paint this bad boy, so gather your painting supplies. Don't forget your hair dryer! Mix some gold paint with water to a fairly thin consistency and brush it all over the lure except for a ½" (13mm) stripe down the center of the belly.

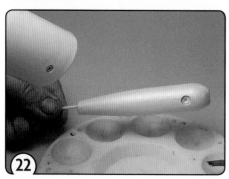

Thoroughly dry this coat with the hair dryer. You can tell when acrylic paint is dry by touching it. When it is dry, it will feel warm to the touch; if it feels cool, than it is not dry. Always dry each and every layer of acrylic—if you do not, the second coat will wash off the previous one.

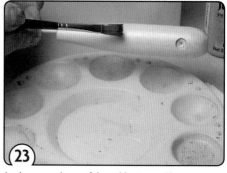

Apply a second coat of the gold mixture. Please note that even with two coats, the paint is still transparent. That is why we thinned the gold with water to a runny consistency. Don't worry if you get the mix too thin—just do a few more coats until it resembles the photo.

**Apply stippling**

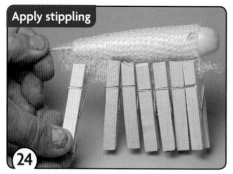

Dry the lure again. Remember that we do not want to emboss the surface or lift off the paint. Cut the netting so that it will wrap around the lure with just a little overlap. Wrap the netting around the lure starting at the head and secure with modified clothespins.

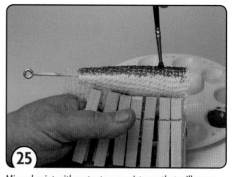

Mix red paint with water to a consistency that will come off the brush easily. After loading a stippling brush, wipe it lightly on a paper towel and stab through the netting. Next, paint one brush width lower down the sides up to the eyehole. Make a final pass about a half brush lower down the side. Repeat the process on the other side.

Mix some of the neon orange color to the same consistency as the red. Load the stippling brush and stab it lightly into the paper towel to remove excess paint. Start at the eyehole and stab toward the tail and back, even with the bottom of the eyehole. Obviously, you will want to repeat these steps on the other side. Dry the paint with your hair dryer. We did not do this between the red and orange because we wanted them to blend slightly.

## *Working with netting*

Notice that this particular netting (pot scrubber variety) is double woven and extra thick. We are not painting scales but rather, small random dots and specks. When brush painting with scale netting of any kind, choose an old, worn-out, short-bristled brush. Use a light touch and stab straight down to the surface.

If the paint coverage looks similar from side to side, remove the netting. Mix some of the green to the same consistency as the red and orange. Wipe off the excess paint and start stippling down the back and down the sides to where the orange specks stop.

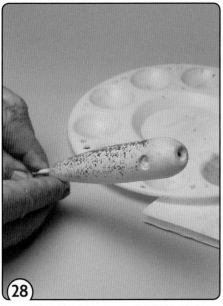

(28)

Repeat this to blend the green so that the back is darker than the sides. In other words, the color fades out as you go from back to belly. As you paint the green, make sure to cover the head and end of the nose. When the green looks good to you, dry the entire lure very well. Remember, the paint should feel warm all over.

**Paint details**

(29)

Mix some black a little thicker than the red. Stipple a line down the center of the back from nose to tail. Note that the line will be made of many little spots. Hold the lure by placing your thumb and forefinger in the eyeholes—it will be easy to locate the center of the back. Give the entire lure a thorough drying.

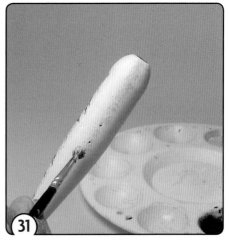

(30)

Load a small pointed brush with the black mixture and stripe the sides and head. These stripes are made with light pressure, an S movement, and a little flick as you pick up the brush. Please note that the head stripes are smaller than those on the body.

(31)

The next step is to mix up some of the tan color and load up the stippling brush. Wipe off the excess and stab a line down the center of the ventral (belly) side from the nose to just behind the hook hanger screw holes. Again, make sure to dry this color completely.

**32** Using a size 0 script-liner brush, load up some of the straight red color and paint in the gill lines. These do not have to be perfectly symmetrical but you do want them close to the same.

**33** Use a fine point permanent ink pen to sign your name to the lure. I recommend you sign all of your work. The painting is now complete but do not reach for the clear coat quite yet.

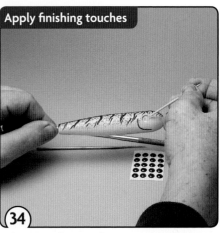

**Apply finishing touches**

**34** Gather up your lure eyes, five-minute epoxy, prick punches, and a toothpick. Mix up a small amount of epoxy with the toothpick and put a little dab in the center of each eyehole.

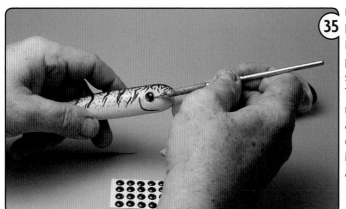

**35** Use the prick punch to lift an eye from the card. Partially insert the eye, put your finger on it, then slide the prick punch out. The eye will go right in, nice and clean. These eyes are self-adhesive, but the epoxy will help hold them in place and seal the wood against water.

fishy fact

**If water visibility is low, fish won't be able to see your lure.**

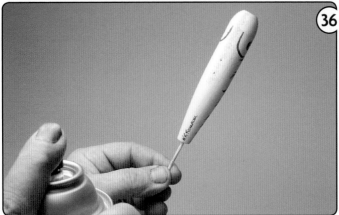

**36** Your signature has had time to dry. Spritz a light coat of the clear finish over it. Let this set up for at least an hour. If you do not do this, the clear coat will make the ink run like a chicken from a weasel. That's right—it won't be pretty!

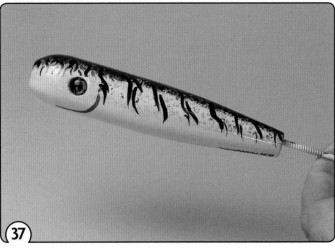

**37**

## Let it cure

If you don't let the clear coat cure hard before you assemble it, you will leave fingerprints all over it, and even cause the finish to slide around on the lure body. Then you get to start all over again.

Apply the first full clear coat. Let this coat set up for a least 30 minutes. An hour would be better. Now give the lure a second clear coat. If the shine is to your liking after about a half-hour, hang it up overnight to cure hard. You could also apply a third coat thirty minutes after the second.

**Install hardware**

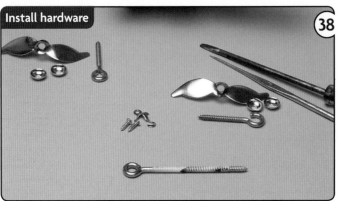

**38** You will now want to gather your hardware, so get the bag you put your parts in and your prick punch, screwdriver, and epoxy.

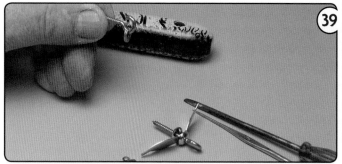

(39) Notice that the eye screw going on the tail end is an open eye. Because we are going to attach the rear hook with a split ring, put that on before you close the eye. Use a pair of your needle-nose pliers to close the screw eye.

(40) Assemble the hardware. It is very easy to turn propellers backward or assemble the cup washers backward. Assemble the rear and front units and lay them down where they will go.

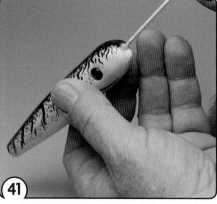

(41) Put epoxy into the nose pilot hole, as well as the countersunk cone.

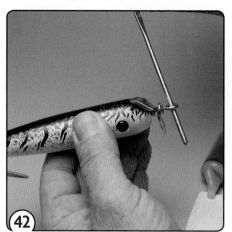

(42) Use your prick punch to tighten the assembly. Back out the screw until the propeller turns freely, but is not sloppy.

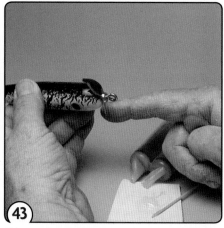

(43) Make sure the eye screw is oriented North/South and not some odd angle. Hit the end of the propeller to make sure that it spins. Follow up by blowing straight onto the prop—it should turn with the force of your breath.

fishy fact: The world's smallest fish, Paedocypris, is 5/16" (7.9mm) long.

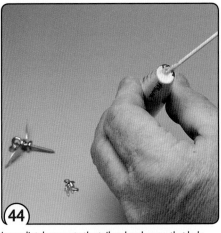

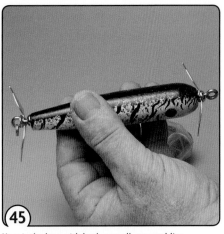

**(44)** Immediately move to the tail end and epoxy that hole and cone the same as the front prop. Make sure the prop spins freely and that the screw eye is aligned.

**(45)** Here is the lure with both propeller assemblies installed, and looking pretty good. We still need to get after that belly hook, however.

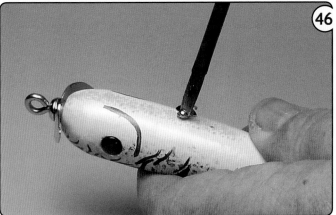

**(46)** Mix a small amount of epoxy and use the toothpick to stuff a little bit into the front hanger screw hole. Install the front hanger screw most of the way but not completely. You will want to be able to move the hanger out to one side.

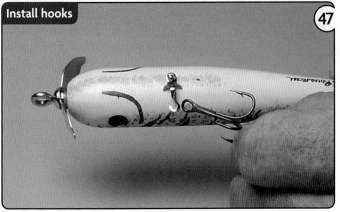

**Install hooks**

**(47)** Slide a size #2 treble hook onto the hanger. Make sure that the hook is oriented with two barbs running along the lure and the other one facing away from the lure body.

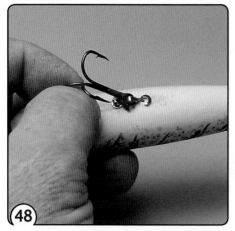

(48) Hold the hook by the third barb and align the hanger with its rear screw hole. Use the toothpick to put a little ball of epoxy into the rear screw hole. Start the screw by hand.

(49) Drive the rear screw in. Go back to the front screw and drive it in. The photo shows the proper installment. The hook orientation will avoid unnecessary wear on the lure body, so be sure yours is correct.

(50) Use the split-ring pliers to start the rear hook into the split ring. The hook orientation does not matter for this type of hook-up. Hold the split ring with your small needle nose pliers and slide the hook around the ring until it is all the way on.

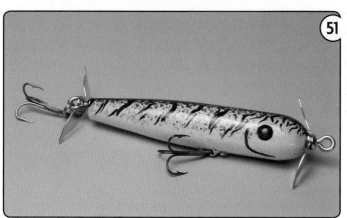

(51) You are now the proud owner of a very fine and classic fishing lure. Here is our finished, hand-painted lure—a long way from the scrap 2 x 4 that we started with.

# LURE 2

# Surface Popper

For our second project, we are going to do another equally classic bass lure: the surface popper. We will use a **purchased body rough-out** and **paint it with common cans of spray paint.** Spray painting produces good lures that also have a unique look to them. By the way, poppers are named for the distinctive noise they make while being retrieved in a stop-and-go manner.

# Surface Popper Pattern

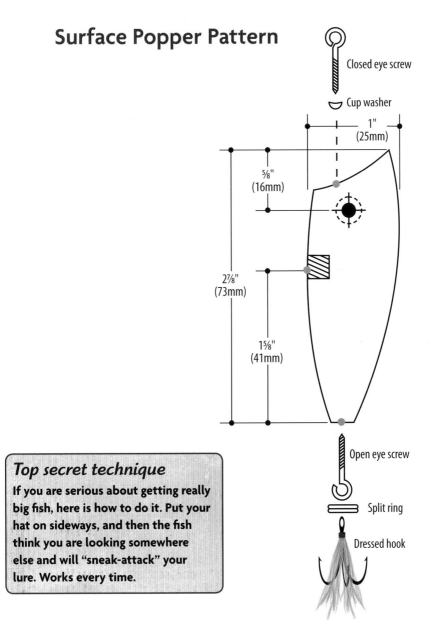

Closed eye screw

Cup washer

1"
(25mm)

⅝"
(16mm)

2⅞"
(73mm)

1⅝"
(41mm)

Open eye screw

Split ring

Dressed hook

> ## Top secret technique
> If you are serious about getting really big fish, here is how to do it. Put your hat on sideways, and then the fish think you are looking somewhere else and will "sneak-attack" your lure. Works every time.

**Photocopy at 100%**

## Materials and tools list

### Materials
- Rough-out lure body, 6" (152mm) musky stick or 3" (76mm) popper
- ¼-ounce non-lead split-shot (counter weight)
- Lure eyes

### Hardware
**Front assembly:**
- Closed eye screw
- Cup washer

**Rear assembly:**
- Open eye screw
- Split ring
- Dressed treble hook (see page 163)

### Tools
- Band saw
- Pencil
- Flexible ruler
- Belt sander or sanding dowel
- Try square
- Handheld power drill
- Brad-point drill bit to match eyes being used
- ¹⁄₁₆" (2mm) twist drill bit
- Countersink bit
- Screwdriver or knife
- 5-minute epoxy
- Toothpick
- Hair dryer
- Coarse fingernail board

- Prick punch
- Cloth and acetone
- Scale netting
- Modified clothespins
- Fine point permanent black marker

### Painting supplies
- Flat white spray paint
- Disposable gloves
- Gold spray paint
- Green spray paint
- Silver metallic spray paint (optional)
- Clear spray finish

### Shape the body

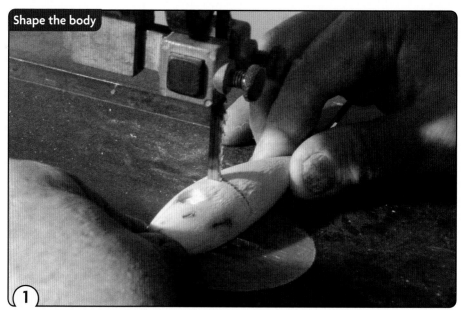

① This project starts with a purchased rough-out body that is already mostly shaped. Cut this body in half at an angle of about 60°, producing two popper bodies. Select one to continue with. Draw a centerline from the uncut tip to the furthest cut point. Remember to lower the blade guard to the proper place—it's raised in this photo so you can see the blade position.

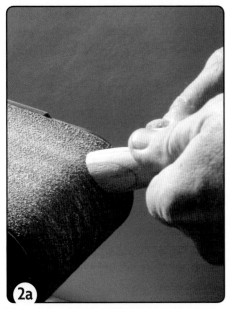

**2a**

We need to sand the face of the popper, and because it also needs to have a cupped face, we'll do both at the same time by sanding with a curved sander. Try the drum end of a belt sander, as pictured.

**2b**

If you do not have a belt sander, than make a homemade sanding stick with a dowel and sandpaper. Please notice that I try to sand at 90° to the centerline of the lure. You may also clamp the stick into a vise and use both hands to control the lure body.

**3**

Here is the face profile we want to achieve. Make sure to reconnect your centerline from back to belly through the center of the face.

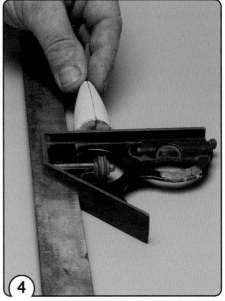

**4**

I like to check that the lure face is square to the length of the lure body using a carpenter's try square.

fishy fact

Coat your fish with oil before you grill to keep the juices in.

57

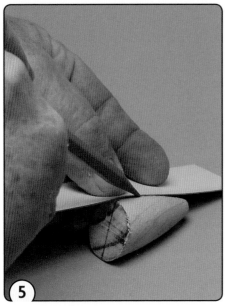

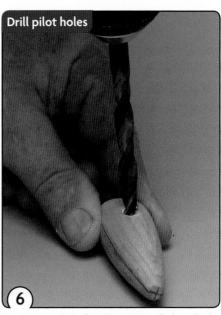

**Drill pilot holes**

**5** After all the sanding, I like to refresh the centerlines. Look at the lure centerlines from all around to visually check that they are correct. It's a lot easier to erase a pencil line than to install your hardware all crooked and have to throw it away and start over.

**6** Transfer the eyeholes from the pattern to the lure. Check that they are symmetrical. Drill the holes with a brad-point bit that matches the eye size. Remember to secure the lure in a bench vise if you don't feel comfortable holding it by hand.

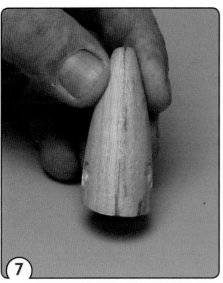

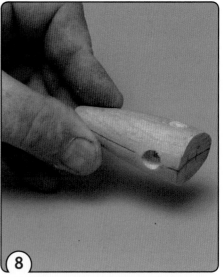

**7** Here you can see the eyes are symmetrical all around. It will serve you well to get into the habit of "rolling the lure" every time you do a layout. This means looking at it from all angles. If anything is amiss it will quickly become obvious.

**8** Here is the hole for the counter weight. The counter weight ensures the lure will float in the right attitude even as it is jerk-retrieved. The hole is drilled with the brad-point bit on the belly centerline and about as far back from the face as the eyes are.

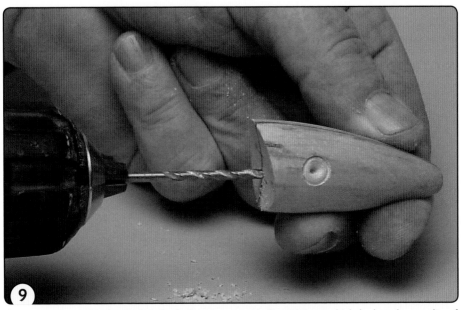

**9**

The next step is to drill in the pilot hole for the front eye screw (the line tie). Locate this hole along the centerline of the face and one-third of the way up from the belly. Use a ¹⁄₁₆" (2mm) twist bit.

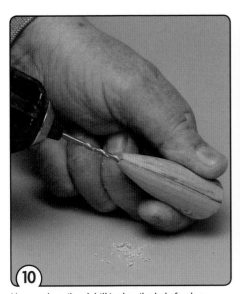

**10**

Move to the tail and drill in the pilot hole for the rear hook screw eye with the same twist bit.

**11**

Use a countersink bit to chamfer the front pilot hole. This makes a nest for the cup washer that will be installed on the finished lure.

**Install counter weights**

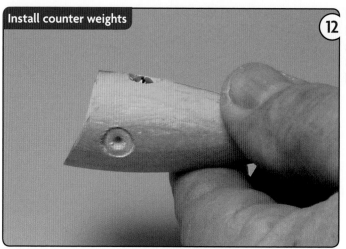

(12) Install the counter weight (a ¼-ounce non-lead split-shot) into the weight hole, making sure it is below the belly's surface.

## Safety warning

Lead is dangerous to your health and also will be illegal in the future, especially on federally controlled waters. Be sure to use non-lead split-shot.

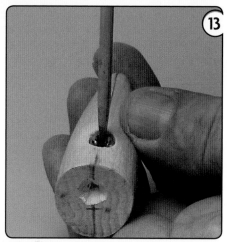

(13) When you have the split-shot inserted, open the split with a screwdriver or knife blade.

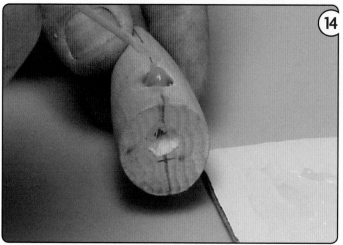

(14) Mix some 5-minute epoxy and fill the hole right over the counter weight. I use a common toothpick to do this because I can work the glue into all the nooks and crannies.

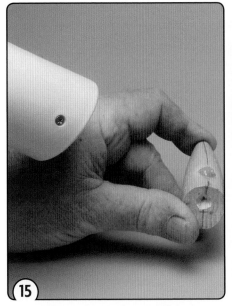

**15** Use a hair dryer to heat up the epoxy. This causes it to become more liquidy and fill the hole. Notice I have placed enough epoxy to form a dome above the belly surface.

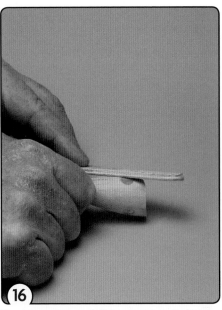

**16** The next step is to sand off the epoxy dome flush with the lure's surface. I use a coarse fingernail board to do it, because it is not aggressive to the wood, yet readily removes the excess epoxy.

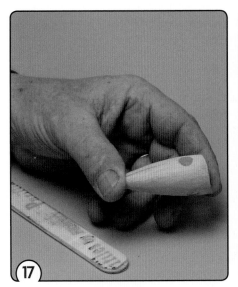

**17** Here is the finished counter weight.

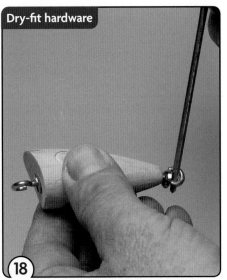

### Dry-fit hardware

**18** Now is the time to dry-fit the hardware. I find it convenient to use my prick punch handle to spin in the eye screws. When dry fitting hardware, always run your screws in nearly snug. Notice how the front cup washer sits nicely in its nest. Now remove all of the hardware.

fishy fact

Surface lures work well over 15 to 25 foot (5 to 8 meter) drop-offs.

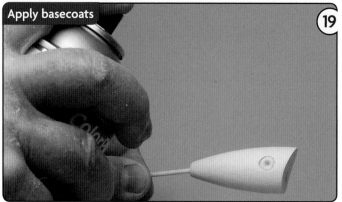

**Apply basecoats**

**19** Give the lure a final sanding and wipe with a damp cloth. I dampen a cloth with acetone to remove all vestiges of sanding dust. Now, paint the entire lure with flat-white primer/base coat, and let it dry overnight.

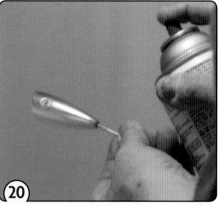

**20** Use your gold spray paint to color the upper half of the lure body. By spraying straight onto the back, only the upper half of the lure will catch the paint.

## Wear gloves

Before we start to paint, I would like to suggest that you get in the habit of wearing disposable gloves while painting. It will be safer for you and save having to wash your hands in thinner. I never got in this habit, so I don't do it, but please do it for your benefit.

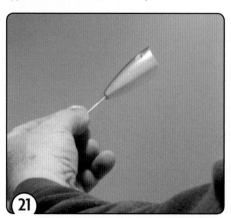

**21** Here you can see how the gold goes just to the center of the lure side and fades toward the belly. This shading occurs by itself when you spray from one direction.

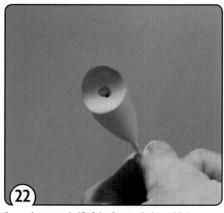

**22** Spray the upper half of the face with the gold. As you look at the lure's face, aim the paint above the lure and let the edge of the spray fan do the work.

**Paint scales**

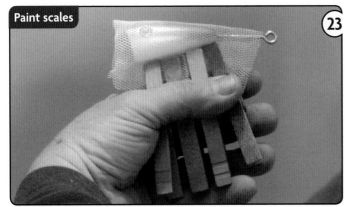

**23** Allow the paint to dry for about an hour. Wrap the lure with some scale netting and secure with your modified clothespins. Until we remove the netting, the clothespins will make a nice handle.

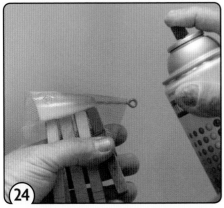

**24** Spray green paint over the gold from straight above. Apply in a series of short puffs—hit the button and immediately release it. Do this from 18" (457mm) away.

## Layering spray paint colors

Step 25 clearly shows the color changing abilities of the color-over-color method. The top of the lure is the same color as the sides, but as the light moves over the curves, the color actually changes. This method will work no matter what base and over-colors you use. Blue over silver, red over gold etc., etc.

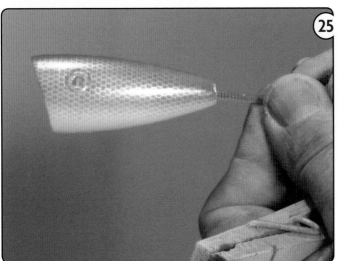

**25** As soon as you are done with the puff painting, remove the netting. Do it carefully so you don't smear the fresh paint. The reason for getting the scale netting off now is you do not want to glue it to the lure as the paint dries.

fishy fact

**Dark surface lures stand out to fish at nighttime.**

**Apply finishing touches**

(26)

If you have dark paint too close to the white belly centerline, you can correct this by puff painting the belly with more white. Make sure to be perpendicular to the belly surface and use a few puffs only.

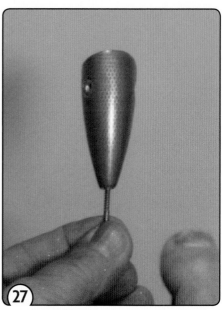

(27)

If you wish to add an extra effect, you can puff the back, belly, or both with silver metallic paint. If you wish to do this, make sure you are at least 24" (610mm) away and give only one, quick puff. Think "less is more."

(28)

Let the lure dry for at least an hour. The paint will be dry to the touch but still "green" (meaning not fully cured), so handle with care. Mix some five-minute epoxy and place a drop in each eyehole. Use your prick punch to lift two eyes and place one into each eyehole.

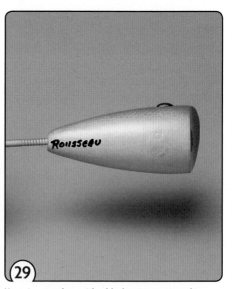

(29)

Now sign your lure with a black permanent marker.

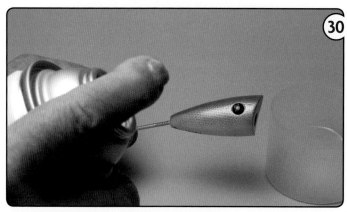

**30** Give the signature two light puffs of clear finish, about 10 minutes apart. Wait 10 minutes. Apply light coats (from at least 18" [457mm] away) to the lure at 20-minute intervals until it's as shiny as you wish. Hang the lure to dry and cure for at least 24 hours. If you do not, you will have fingerprints imbedded forever into your lure.

**Install hardware**

## Glue the screws

Anytime you put a screw into a lure, make sure to put a little glue into the hole first with a toothpick. This is not to hold in the screw. Adding glue lubricates the screw as it cuts into the wood and helps to seal out water.

**31** Always lay your hardware out to check the proper order of installation and save yourself some trouble. When you are satisfied everything is correct, install the hardware.

**32** Here is our finished lure. It's as nice as any and you had the pleasure of making it yourself. This particular lure is really effective on largemouth bass, and in the spring, Northern pike will attack it without mercy!

fishy act    Try blue and green lures for bass.

## LURE 3
# Perch Crawler

For our third project, we'll make a perch crawler. This is a surface bait used mostly for bass, but is equally deadly for spring pike and musky. A crawler has a bib at the front that makes a "plop, plop, plop" noise when retrieved. We will be making the lure from a **dowel rod** and painting it with an **airbrush**.

# Perch Crawler Pattern

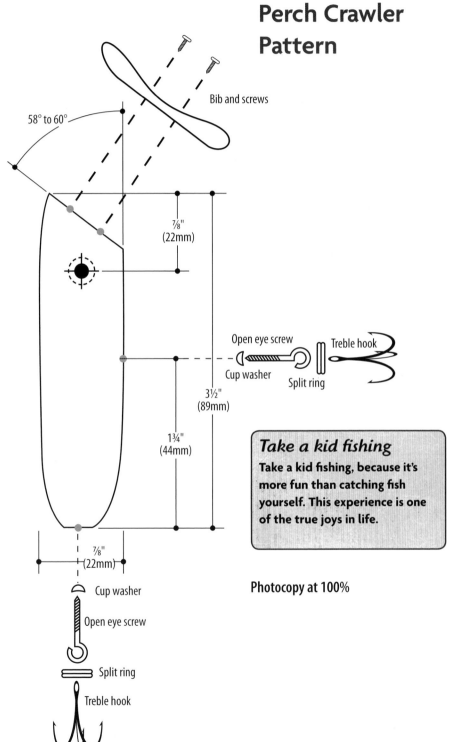

Bib and screws

58° to 60°

⅞"
(22mm)

Open eye screw

Cup washer

Treble hook

Split ring

3½"
(89mm)

1¾"
(44mm)

⅞"
(22mm)

Cup washer

Open eye screw

Split ring

Treble hook

## Take a kid fishing

**Take a kid fishing, because it's more fun than catching fish yourself. This experience is one of the true joys in life.**

**Photocopy at 100%**

# Materials and tools list

## Materials
- ¾" (19mm) -diameter poplar dowel
- 3-D lure eyes

## Hardware
**Front assembly:**
- Bib and screws

**Belly assembly:**
- Open eye screw
- Split ring
- Treble hook

**Rear assembly:**
- Open eye screw
- Cup washer
- Treble hook

## Tools
- Belt sander, knife, or sanding block
- Band saw
- Pencil
- Flexible plastic ruler
- Handheld power drill
- Countersink bit
- ¹⁄₁₆" (2mm) twist bit
- Brad-point bit
- Prick punch
- Painting handle (eye screw)
- 5-minute epoxy
- Toothpick
- Fine point black permanent marker

## Painting supplies
- Flat-white spray paint
- Airbrush
- 600-grit sandpaper
- Rag
- Acetone
- Lacquer airbrush paints: glimmer gold, transparent light green, black umber, perch orange
- White poster board or cardboard
- Scale netting
- Modified clothespins
- Clear spray finish

### Shape the body

**1** Grab a piece of dowel to start this lure. In this case, I chose a ¾" (19mm)-diameter poplar dowel.

**2** Taper one end of the dowel. I'm using a belt sander here, but you can do it just as easily with a knife, or even a homemade sanding block, as we did in the first project. The end we taper will be the tail.

**3** We are now going to cut the face off with the band saw. Because we're making a crawler, we cut at an angle of 60–70° to accommodate the bib. The exact angle makes small differences in the way the crawler acts, so check your pattern to be sure. Remember to lower the blade guard to the proper place—it's raised in this photo so you can see the blade position.

**4** Sand the face flat. This is a perfect time to make changes to the angle if you want to. Again, I'm using the belt sander, but the heavy sanding block works just great as well. After sanding, check to see that the face is square to the lure (i.e., at 90° to the long axis).

### Record the angle

If you make a crawler that performs to your exact desires, make a note of the angle and write it on your pattern sheet so you can duplicate the sweet action.

**Lay out guidelines**

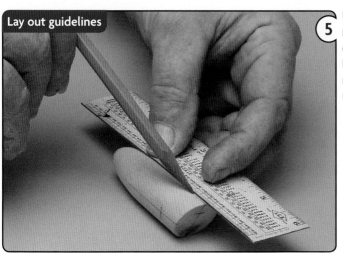

**5** Use the flexible plastic ruler to mark in all of your centerlines. Make sure to look over the entire lure to make sure everything lines up well and looks good.

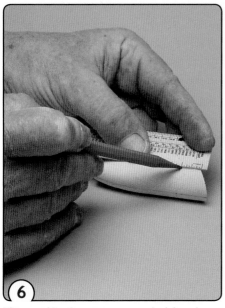

**6**

After consulting the pattern, measure back from the face along the eye line to locate the eyeholes.

**7**

Using the bib, line up the screw holes with the face centerline. Make sure the line-tie hole is not obstructed by the body. Mark the screw holes on the centerline. Note that the lure is shown here belly-up (the bib is upside down)— the line tie hole goes on top of the lure.

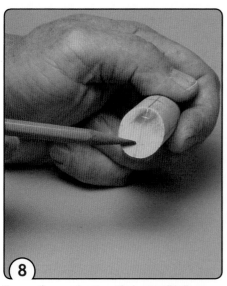

**8**

Here are the screw locations. The lure is still belly up.

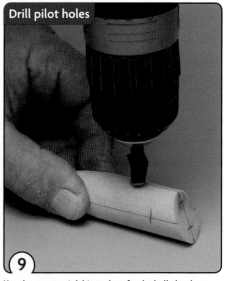

**Drill pilot holes**

**9**

Use the countersink bit to chamfer the belly hook screw location. This does two things at once. First, it helps center the small pilot hole drill bit. Second, it makes a nest for the cup washer we will be using. Remember to secure the lure in a bench vise if you don't feel comfortable holding it by hand.

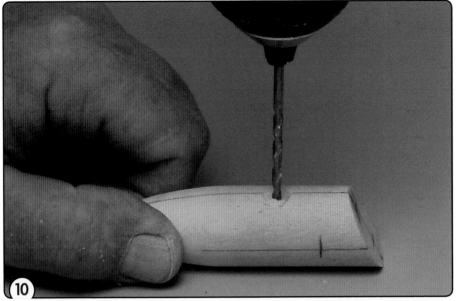

10 Drill in the belly hook pilot hole with a ¹⁄₁₆" (2mm) twist bit. The countersink hole will help keep the pilot bit from walking off center. While we are at it, let's drill in the pilot hole for the rear hook mount screw as well.

11 Now it's time to drill in the eyeholes. Use a brad-point bit that matches the eye size. On surface lures, I like to have the eyes slightly bug-eyed, so drill the eyeholes a little shallow.

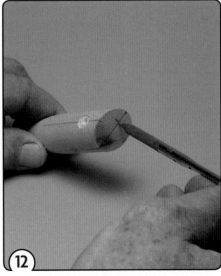

12 The screws for mounting the bib are fairly small, so don't use the drill for the pilot holes. Instead, use your prick punch and stab the holes in. As with drilling a hole, make sure to stab in perpendicular to the surface and parallel to the long centerline.

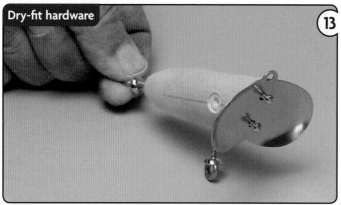

**Dry-fit hardware**

**13** Dry-fit your hardware and make sure there are no problems. Run all of the screws in about 90%, but not tight. Here you can see how the line-tie hole nicely clears the lure's body.

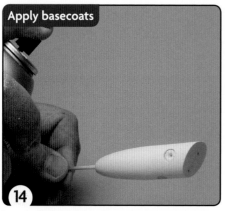

**Apply basecoats**

**14** Remove the hardware and screw in a painting handle. Spray on one to three coats of flat-white primer. Let the primer dry overnight.

## A note on airbrushing

Because we are going to airbrush this lure, make sure the primer and paints are compatible. For example, don't put an enamel coat underneath lacquer paint. It is equally important to lightly sand the primer with fine sandpaper (600 grit) and wipe off the dust with a rag dampened in the correct thinner. In this case, that would be acetone.

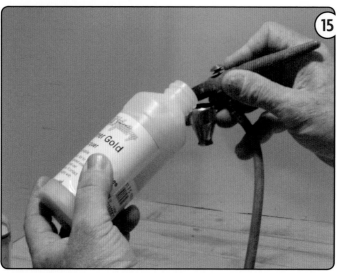

**15** To start our perch paint job, we will use glimmer gold as our color base coat. Fill one-third of the airbrush's cup with gold paint.

**16** Fill the remainder of the cup with pure acetone to thin the paint.

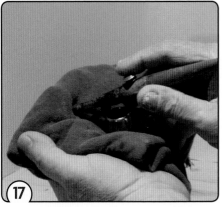

**17** Use an absorbent rag to cover the tip of the airbrush, and under the cup. Press the trigger. This causes the air to back-flush through the cup and mix the paint and acetone.

## Blending colors

By mixing our paint really thin, we are, in effect, blending colors right on the lure. You can always add a couple of thin layers, but one that is too thick means you get to wipe everything off and start over again. So I have what I call the standard mix: one part paint to two parts thinner.

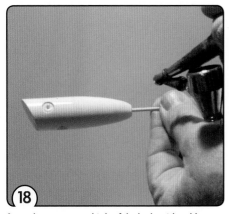

**18** Spray the upper two-thirds of the body with gold paint—leave the belly white for now. You may need more than one coat. Thin is better than too thick.

**Paint scales**

**19** The second color is transparent light green. Add the paint and acetone—one part paint to two parts acetone—and use the rag to back-flush the paint.

 fishy fact · **When the dogwood blooms, crappie fishing is good!**

Always keep a piece of white poster board or cardboard pinned up in your paint area. This is handy for checking your airbrush adjustments and color intensity. If the board is conveniently placed, you will actually use it. Test the green color until you are pleased with it.

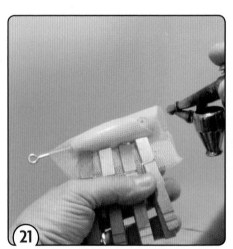

Wrap the lure with a piece of scale netting and secure with modified clothespins. Spray over the gold with the transparent green. You will see a greenish-gold color start to develop. The exact shade of this color is up to your personal taste—you control the shade, not the paint.

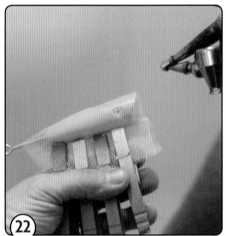

Give the back a few more coats of the green to establish a color difference between the back and the flanks (sides). Note that even though the bib is going to cover the entire front of the lure, I paint that area also, simply to help protect the wood.

**Paint stripes**

(23) We are now going to darken the back, so load up some black umber (a warm brownish black). This time, however, mix in a little more acetone. Use one part paint to three parts thinner. Use the back-flush mixing technique.

(24) Adjust your spray to a fine line and shoot some paint on the cardboard. You can shoot right over your transparent green test strip to get a feel for how the two colors will look on the lure. Notice that I first adjust the line width (top lines) and then check for color (lower part).

(25) Spray a narrow dark line down the middle of the back. It should be a little narrower than the green contrast line.

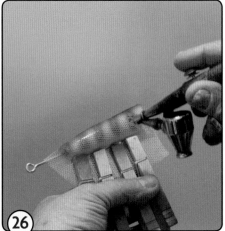

(26) Use the same black umber to lay out your side stripes. Perch usually have seven stripes, but really, fish can't count anyway, so just make as many as you think looks good. On this size lure, I make five. Notice how light the first coat is; this is good!

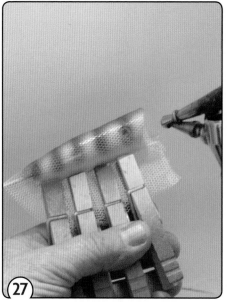

Give your stripes a second (or third) coat. Since it's nearly impossible to follow the first marks exactly, the stripes turn out nicely shaded and real looking. That is why we paint them in layers instead of a single dark stripe. When you complete both sides, remove the scale netting by teasing it away slowly and carefully.

Here is the lure with the netting removed. Hey, I really did the other side, too! Our next color is lighter than black umber, so we need to clean the paint cup thoroughly. Dump any excess and fill the cup with acetone. Back-flush it good and then spray all of the acetone out through the tip.

**Paint the belly**

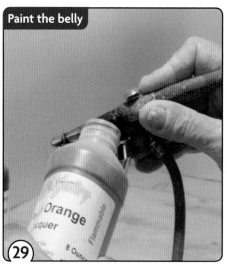

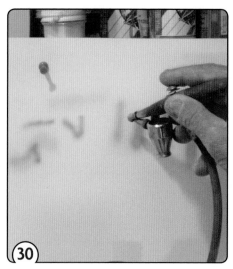

We are now ready to mix some perch orange color. Use the standard 1:2 ratio, mixed in the cup—well, heck, you know the routine.

Adjust the spray fan to a fine line and test it on the cardboard.

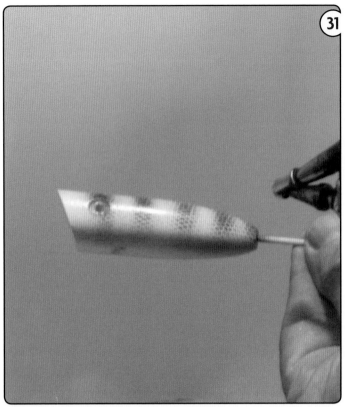

**31** We will paint a thin orange stripe along the bottom of the gold-green. Make sure to leave a thin white belly stripe—painting white back over the orange is a real pain. Be patient with these two stripes and carefully give them two to three coats until you have a nice intense color value.

## Apply finishing touches

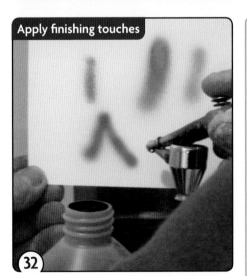

**32** Drain the excess orange into the bottle. Load and mix some black umber like we always do. The umber is so dark, any residual orange will not bother the mix. Set your spray fan to a medium width and test it.

## Saving paint

An airbrush cup only holds about ¹⁄₁₆th of an ounce, so when leftover paint is returned to the bottle, it will not dilute the paint much. Keep in mind that acetone evaporates into the air very rapidly, and so the original paint stays so close to its original consistency that any worries about diluting the paint become moot. I have done it this way for more than 20 years and never had any paint go bad. I originally did it this way to conserve paint.

**33** Lightly spray down the center of the back. This will do two things. First, it will tone down and cover the scales on the top of the back, and second, it will blend the stripes into the back color. This photo clearly shows where the back scales are covered. Let the lure dry for about an hour.

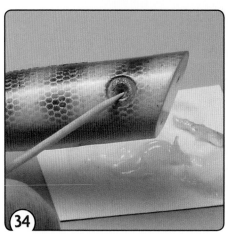

**34** Mix some five-minute epoxy with a toothpick and place a small drop in the center of the eyehole. Though we have let the lure dry for an hour, the paint is not cured, so handle the lure with care.

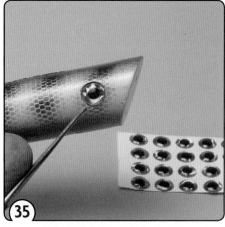

**35** Use your prick punch to lift a 3-D eye from the card and install it into the eyehole, directly on top of the epoxy drop.

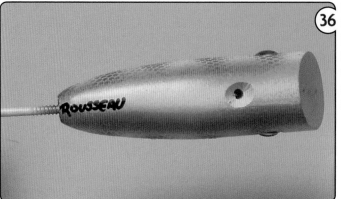

**36** Use a permanent marker to autograph your lure. Please remember to seal the signature by puff-coating some clear spray over it and letting it dry about 20 minutes.

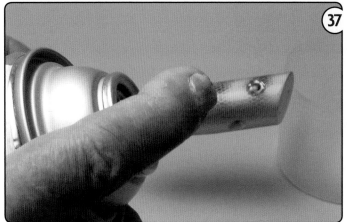

**37** Now clear-coat the entire lure. Use two to three light coats spaced 20 minutes apart. Remember, light coats dry faster and build shine faster than heavy coats do. Let the paint job cure by drying it for 24 hours.

## Install hardware

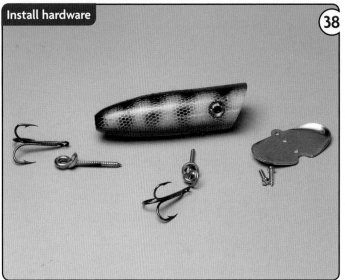

**38** Lay out your hardware exactly how it will be installed on the lure. Notice the belly hook is attached with a split ring and the tail hook will mount directly to the screw eye.

**39** Here is our finished dowel rod. Heck, if I was a bass, I'd bite it!

fishy fact

**Try fishing deep water along the bend in a river.**

## LURE 4
# Saltwater Flatfish

A flatfish is a lure that is ovoid in section and has a pronounced upward hump in the back. Imagine an oval stick of clay you've pushed upward in the middle. They usually have a sloped and cupped face to make them wiggle. This lure is in the family of floater-divers. I've created this lure from **scrap wood** and painted it with an **airbrush**. This lure can be cast on inshore waters or fished deep by down-rigging or wire-lining. While this lure is made for saltwater, it is also effective in the Great Lakes when fished for king salmon. I guess they don't know they aren't in the ocean anymore!

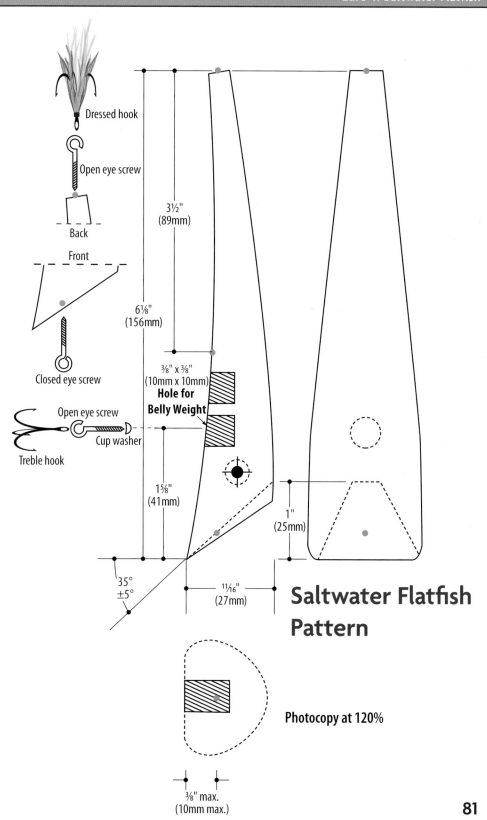

Dressed hook

Open eye screw

Back

Front

6⅛"
(156mm)

3½"
(89mm)

Closed eye screw

Open eye screw

Treble hook

Cup washer

⅜" x ⅜"
(10mm x 10mm)
**Hole for Belly Weight**

1⅝"
(41mm)

1"
(25mm)

35°
±5°

¹¹⁄₁₆"
(27mm)

# Saltwater Flatfish Pattern

**Photocopy at 120%**

⅜" max.
(10mm max.)

## Materials and tools list

### Materials
- 2 by 4 scrap
- 3-D lure eyes
- ¼" (6mm) steel rod (counter weights)

### Hardware
**Front assembly:**
- Closed eye screw

**Belly assembly:**
- Open eye screw
- Cup washer
- Treble hook

**Rear assembly:**
- Dressed treble hook (see page 163)

### Tools
- Band saw
- Pencil
- Masking tape
- Flexible ruler
- Sanding block
- Hack saw
- 5-minute epoxy
- Coarse fingernail board
- Handheld power drill
- ¼" (6mm) -diameter twist drill bit
- ¹⁄₁₆" (2mm) -diameter twist drill bit
- Bit to match diameter of eyes
- 600- to 800-grit sandpaper
- 5-minute epoxy

- Toothpick
- Prick punch
- Fine point permanent marker

### Painting supplies
- Flat white spray paint
- Airbrush
- Lacquer paints for airbrush: silver metallic, transparent marlin blue, black umber, cover white
- Acetone
- Cardboard
- Clear spray finish

**Shape the body**

1

Lay out your pattern, both top and side views, on a piece of 2 by 4 scrap wood. Start by cutting the proper width for the top view. Discard the unused portion. Remember to lower the blade guard to the proper place—it's raised in this photo so you can see the blade position.

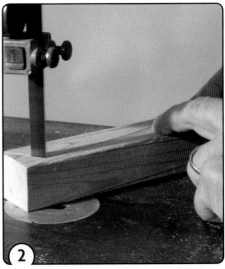

2

Make your first lure cut by going up the face. Do not cut through the block, simply cut the pattern line and stop.

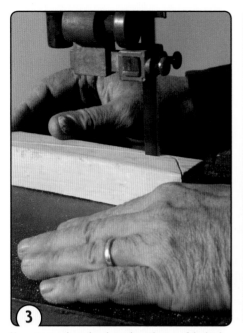

**3**

Now, start at the tail and cut along the top of the back until you reach the face cut. You want the entire top of the block to come off in one piece. Set this piece aside and save it.

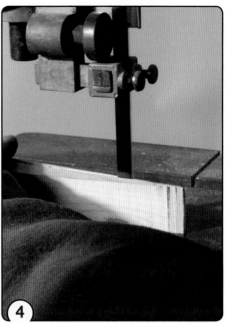

**4**

Cut the belly line and remove the entire bottom of the block in one single piece. Save this piece as well.

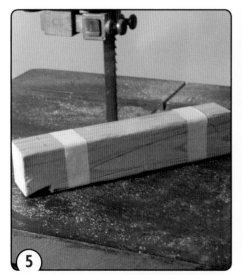

**5**

Replace the top and bottom pieces in their original position and secure them with masking tape. Notice you can see the pattern right through the tape. You can also safely saw right through it. See where this is going?

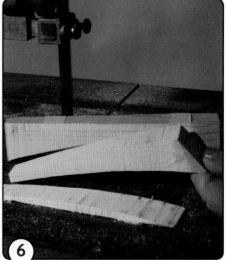

**6**

Cut out the top view while the tape holds it together for you. The reason for the taping is the complicated curves of this lure. All of the surfaces are curved; taping the block back together ensures you will start out with a lure shape that has a square top, bottom, and sides.

fishy fact

Stay away from murky waters if night fishing for bass.

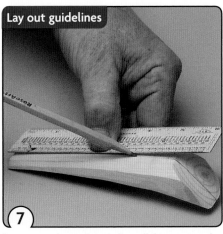

**Lay out guidelines**

**7** Draw on your long axis centerlines all the way around the lure, including the face.

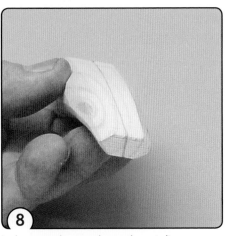

**8** Look over your lure to make sure the centerlines are correct and everything looks good. Notice I have sanded the sharp corners off the back to start rounding it.

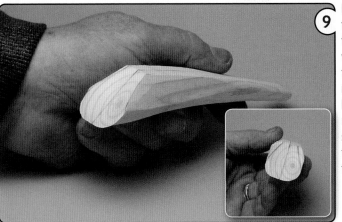

**9** Pencil in the final shape on the face (see inset). At the face, these flat final cuts will be as shown, but as they progress toward the rear, they will fade away by the time they reach mid-lure. Here you can see where the face cuts fade out before you get to the tail.

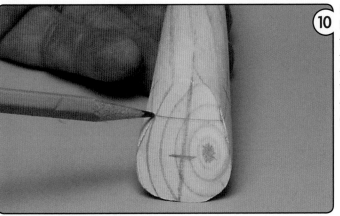

**10** Rough-sand the general body shape. Mark the line tie screw hole (lower X); the upper line is to mark the height of the eye line. You will want this line to be truly horizontal, meaning 90° to the centerline.

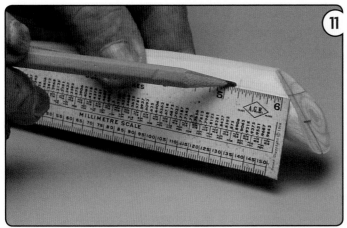

**11** Use your flexible ruler to mark a line from the center of the tail to the eye line at the face. At the same time, measure from the face back to the center of the eye location and mark an X. In this case, it is marked ¾" (19mm) back from the face.

## Install counter weights

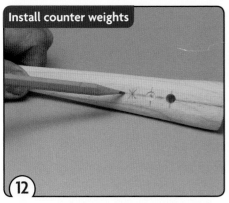

**12** This lure is going to have two counter weights and a belly hook eye screw. Try to get in the habit of X-ing the screw hole so you don't make a mistake while drilling the different hole sizes. Drill the counter weight holes with a ¼" (6mm) drill bit.

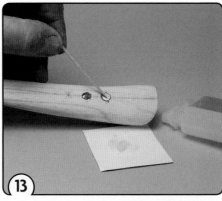

**13** Dry-fit the counter weights—¼" (6mm) steel rod cut with a hacksaw. Make the holes deep enough. Notice the front weight is not deep enough, while the rear one is correct. Secure the weights with five-minute epoxy. Make sure to leave your epoxy domed.

## Drill pilot holes

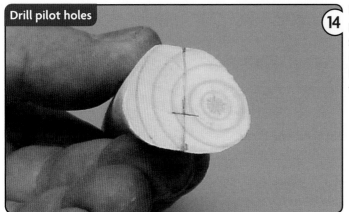

**14** It is now time to drill the pilot holes for the eye screws using the ⅟₁₆" (2mm) twist bit. Here I have started at the face and the line-tie location.

Trace a figure 8 with surface baits to encourage a strike.

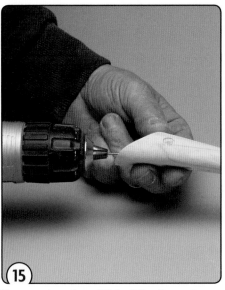

**(15)**

Please note the angle at which I'm drilling. You want to go on an up angle so that your line tie screw misses the steel counter weight. Drill in your belly and tail pilot holes, too. Make sure you drill these right down the center of the lure. Remember to secure the lure in a bench vise if you don't feel comfortable holding it by hand.

### Dry-fit hardware

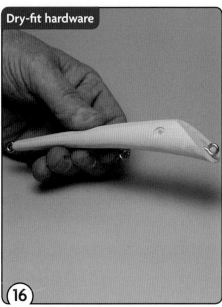

**(16)**

Now is the time to drill the eyeholes. Use a bit that matches the size eye you will use. Dry-fit the hardware. Remember not to run the screws all the way home and tight. Notice how heavy the hardware is for a saltwater lure and that it is stainless steel to boot.

### Apply basecoats

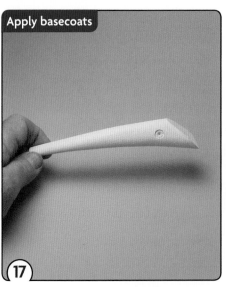

**(17)**

We will need at least three coats of the flat white base coat. You will want to sand and wipe between coats, so wait about one-half hour between each coat. Using 600- to 800-grit paper will be sufficient. Make sure to let this base coat cure overnight.

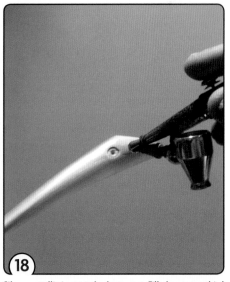

**(18)**

Silver metallic is our color base coat. Fill about one-third of the cup with the silver. Fill the rest of the cup with acetone. Back flush (see page 73 for more instruction). Paint the upper two-thirds of the body (not the belly) with the silver mixture until you have an even coat of color.

Our next color will be transparent marlin blue. Use our standard mix—one part paint to two parts thinner—and back flush as before. Set your airbrush spray fan to a medium-wide pattern and test it on your cardboard.

Spray a light, even coat of blue over the silver. The silver will show through, creating a silvery-blue color. The exact shade is your choice: the more blue you use, the darker it becomes. I prefer a lighter blue shade to give me more contrast later on.

**Paint stripes**

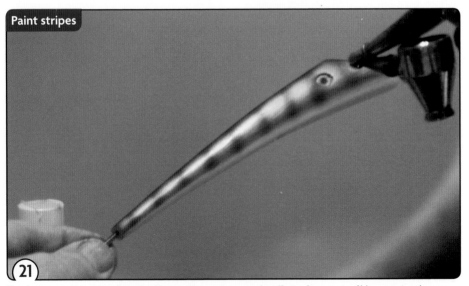

Use the same paint to start the stripes' layout. Here you can see the effects of two coats of blue covering the silver—that's why I opt for the lighter silver blue on the background.

fishy fact — **Use small lures in weedy waters.**

22 Use the blue to give the back a third and fourth coat. You want a narrow dark line running down the center of the back. This step gives contrast and helps blend the stripes and back together.

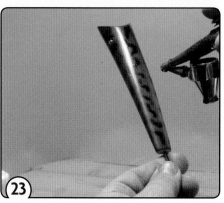

Our third color will be black umber. Use our standard paint-to-thinner ratio and mixing technique. Set your spray fan to a very thin line and then test it on the cardboard. Start on the back and make a series of small worm-shaped marks down the center of the entire back.

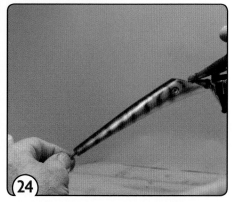

Now we want to make worm stripes directly over the blue stripes we roughed in earlier on the sides. Notice the black is narrower than the blue stripe lines; this makes it much easier to place worm marks over the straight blue stripes.

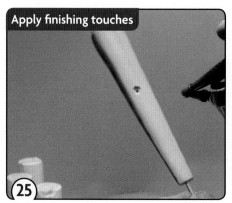

**Apply finishing touches**

We will be using cover white, so clean out the brush tip and cup with thinner. Paint the belly a nice bright white, using perhaps three to four coats. We want a high contrast between the belly and the body.

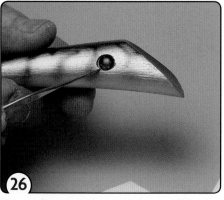

Mix some five-minute epoxy and place a small drop in the eyeholes. Use your prick punch to set the 3-D eyes. Use red eyes for contrast or silver for realism.

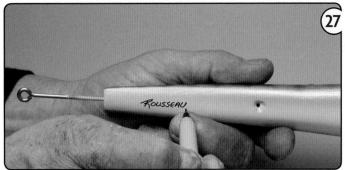

**27** Don't forget to sign your lure. I know that the signing, sealing, etc., gets to be a real chore, but remember the gallery photographs that said "unknown Michigan maker"? Please take the time to do this.

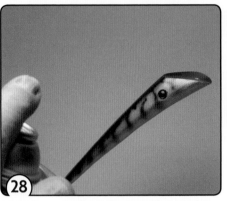

**28** Give your signature the regular two puff coats of clear finish to seal the ink, wait 30 minutes, and then clear coat the lure with two to three light coats.

### Install hardware

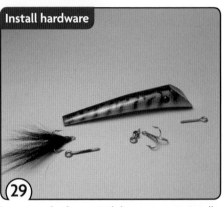

**29** Lay out your hardware exactly how you want to install it. Note that I'm going to use the painting screw on the lure. This helps seal the screw. Now, install the hardware. Apply epoxy in the screw holes to help seal the wood from water infiltration.

**30** Here is the finished flatfish, which hardly resembles the 2 by 4 piece of scrap we started with.

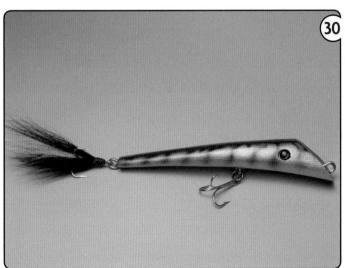

fishy fact **Try fire-tiger colors for muskie day fishing, and red or orange at dusk.**

# LURE 5
# Floating-Diving Minnow

Let's do our next lure in the floating-diving minnow style. Grab some **scrap wood** and your **airbrush** for this one! This lure is painted as a young largemouth bass. Because this lure represents a fingerling, it is effective on most predator species including bass, walleyes, Northern pike, and even on some large perch.

# Floating-Diving Minnow Pattern

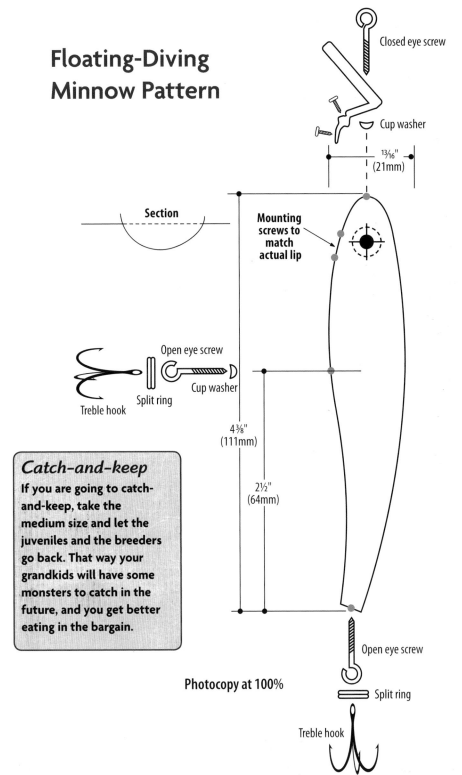

Closed eye screw

Cup washer

$^{13}/_{16}$"
(21mm)

Section

Mounting
screws to
match
actual lip

Open eye screw

Cup washer

Treble hook

Split ring

$4^{3}/_{8}$"
(111mm)

$2^{1}/_{2}$"
(64mm)

## Catch-and-keep

If you are going to catch-and-keep, take the medium size and let the juveniles and the breeders go back. That way your grandkids will have some monsters to catch in the future, and you get better eating in the bargain.

Photocopy at 100%

Open eye screw

Split ring

Treble hook

# Materials and tools list

## Materials
- ¾" (19mm) scrap lumber from a 1 by 4 or 1 by 2
- 3-D lure eyes

## Hardware
**Front assembly:**
- Closed eye screw
- Cup washer
- Diving lip and screws

**Belly assembly:**
- Open eye screw
- Split ring
- Treble hook

**Rear assembly:**
- Open eye screw
- Split ring
- Treble hook

## Tools
- Band saw
- Pencil
- Flexible ruler
- Prick punch
- Handheld power drill
- Brad-point drill bit to match eye size
- Utility knife
- Coarse fingernail foam board

- Sandpaper
- Rag
- 5-minute epoxy
- Toothpick
- Fine point permanent black marker

## Painting supplies
- Flat white base coat spray
- Airbrush
- Lacquer paints: glimmer gold, transparent light green, medium green, black umber, cover white
- Acetone
- Cardboard

### Cut out the body

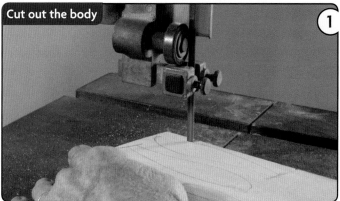

**1** Usually, I use ¾" (19mm) scrap lumber (1 by 4, 1 by 2, etc.) to build my minnow lures. Trace your pattern (page 91) on the scrap and cut it out. Notice that if you lay the patterns out head to tail you can get more lures from the board. Remember to lower the blade guard to the proper place—it's raised in this photo so you can see the blade position.

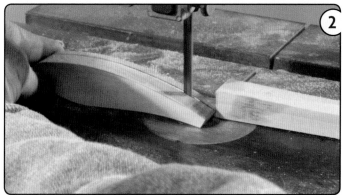

**2** Rip the wood down to ½" (13mm) thick. Use a push stick.

## Lay out guidelines

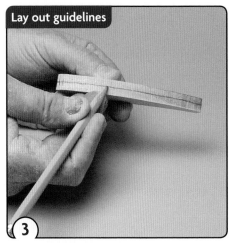

**3**

Draw the long axis centerlines. Hold the pencil between the index finger and the thumb. Place the pencil tip on the centerline mark, and place the middle finger against the edge of the wood. Without changing anything, simply trace around the lure.

## Quick pattern template

Notice that the ¼" (6mm) piece of scrap would make an excellent pattern and is easier to trace around than paper. Clean it up a little, mark what it is, and pitch it into the pattern box!

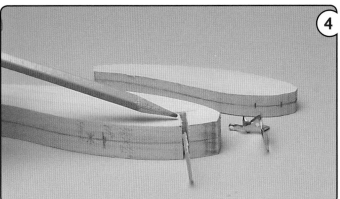

**4** I've chosen a screw-on lip for the lure (back). Use the lip to mark the mounting screw locations on the centerline. The lip goes on the belly side at the nose. If you choose a glue-in lip, cut the lip slot at this time with the band saw—it is easy to keep everything squared up this way, but not if you wait!

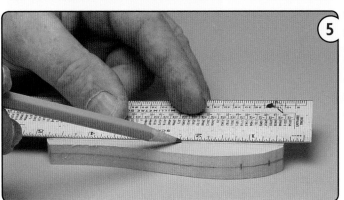

**5** You will need to draw in an eye line. Make this by connecting the center of the nose to the center of the tail with a ruled pencil line. Do I really have to tell you to do it on both sides? Nah.

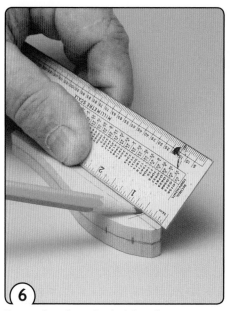

(6)

Measure along the eye line back from the nose to locate the center of the eyehole. In this case, we are ½" (13mm) behind the nose. I like to locate my minnow eyes near the nose because it makes the bait look more juvenile. If you set the eye a little further back, the bait looks more adult.

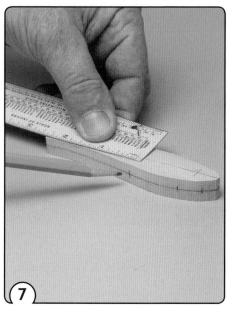

(7)

Here we are locating our belly hook location. Choose this location carefully so that this hook will not tangle up on the lip or the rear hook. Retrieving a lure with hung hooks will get you madder than a wet hen, and do it in a hurry too!

### Drill pilot holes

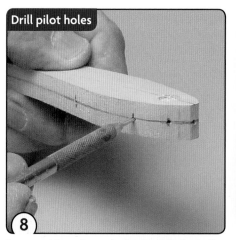

(8)

Use your prick punch to make the pilot holes for the lip mounting screws. These are small enough that pilot hole drill bits are too big in diameter. Notice I have drilled starter eyeholes. I call them that because as we round out the body, we will need to refresh them.

### Shape the body

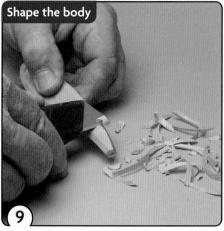

(9)

So far, we have shaped our lures by using various sanders. It is just as easy (if not easier) to shape by carving with your utility knife, as in this photograph.

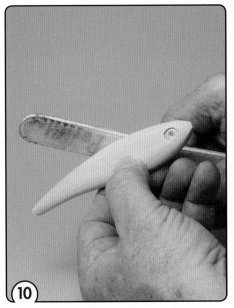

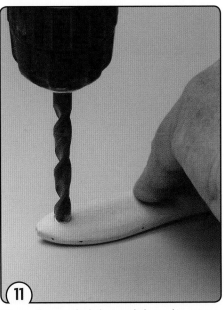

**10** After carving the body, smooth it out with a coarse fingernail foam board. Notice the eyeholes are shallow at the front and bottom. This is why we need to refresh them.

**11** It is now time to refresh those eyeholes, making sure they are straight to the body. While you are at it, it might be good time to refresh yourself with a beverage of choice. Remember to secure the lure in a bench vise if you don't feel comfortable holding it by hand.

**Dry-fit hardware**

**Apply basecoats**

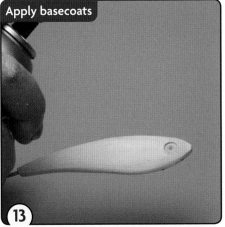

**12** Dry-fit your hardware to make sure everything is looking good, is on center, and without "oopsies." That is a word that can come up after a few beverages! Like always, do not run your screws down tight.

**13** Remove all of the hardware except for the tail screw, which will be our painting handle, and give the lure two to three coats of flat white base coat. Remember, 20 minutes between coats, and dry overnight. The next day, sand lightly and wipe with a damp rag.

 **fishy fact** Isinglass, from fish swimbladders, is used to clarify beer.

**14** This paint scheme is going to look like a largemouth bass, so load your airbrush with glimmer gold in the usual manner. Set the spray fan to a medium-width fan and shoot in the upper two-thirds of the body, leaving the belly white.

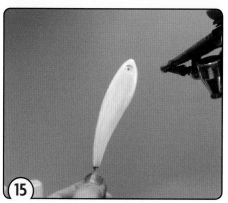

**15** Now give the body a second coat of the gold to produce a nice light but even tone. This photograph shows the approximate color you are looking for.

## Why lacquer?

The main reason I use lacquer paint is this: By the time you have painted the other side, the first side is already dry enough to repaint. Acetone flashes off that fast.

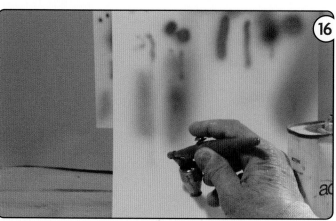

**16** Load and mix a batch of transparent light green in the standard method. Adjust your spray fan to a medium to small fan and check it on the cardboard.

**17** Paint over the gold with the transparent green. The resulting color looks almost chartreuse because you are seeing both the gold and the green at the same time. Notice my hand is a poster child for why you may wish to wear disposable gloves. Just because I'm a dummy is no reason for you to be!

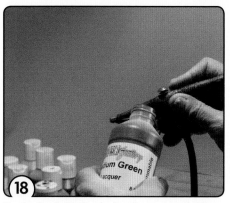

**18** Now load and mix a batch of medium green color. You will want to mix this with more thinner, so make your ratio 1:3. You can always put more on, but if you make this too dark, you get to start all over again!

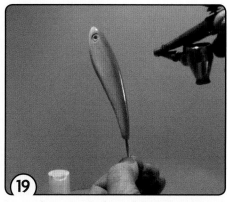

**19** Do not adjust your spray fan at all. Paint the center of the back until you achieve a band that looks like a darker version of the sides (flanks). The photograph is a fair way to judge this color differential.

Paint detail

**20** Add a little black umber color to the paint you already have loaded (back flush to mix). Don't worry; you can't make it too dark. Now adjust the fan to a fine line and make sure to test the setting on the cardboard.

fishy fact

"Men and fish get in trouble when they open their mouths."

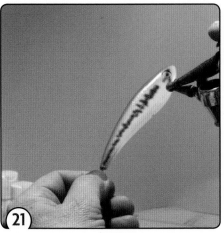

Start by roughing in the irregular band along the lateral line and put a couple of horizontal bars through the eyeholes. Note that the side and eye marks are not critical as to shape, but they are the defining marks on a young bass.

Give the lateral line a second coat, and also paint a dark narrow band down the center of the back.

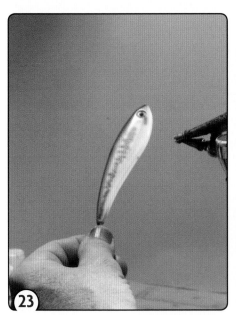

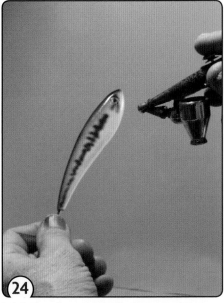

Thoroughly clean your airbrush and reload it with cover white in the standard 1:2 ratio. Set the spray fan to a medium-to-small line. Use the white to repaint the belly. Another defining feature of young bass is their snow-white belly.

Lightly clean the cup out and load up some glimmer gold. Paint over the sides and back with a light coat. This step blends all of the colors together. Keep it light and remember that less is more.

**Install eyes and hardware**

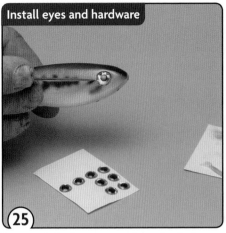

(25)

Mix up some 5-minute epoxy and put a drop in the centers of the eyeholes. Use the prick punch to mount the 3-D eyes. Here I have used gold eyes for the realistic look but red eyes are also productive as a contrast color.

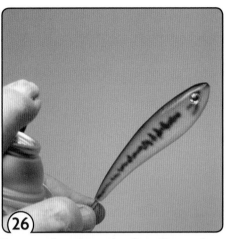

(26)

Use your marker to sign your lure. Remember to set the ink with a couple of puff coats of clear finish from 18" (457mm). Hang the lure up for about 30 minutes; then, spray the entire lure with two to three light coats of clear about 20 minutes apart. Hang it up to cure for 24 hours.

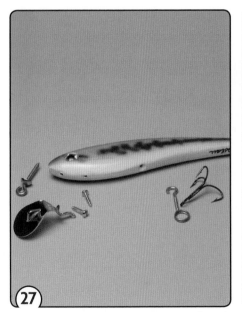

(27)

Lay out your hardware in the same order you will install it. There are two line ties on this lure: an eye screw at the nose and the one on the diving lip itself. I do this because I like to be able to change the running depth while fishing. If a glue-in plastic lip is desired, I install it as the very last thing.

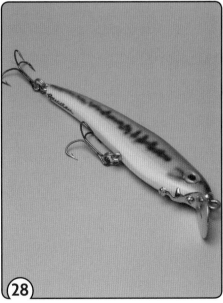

(28)

The bass fingerling is ready to get bit. I did not use the scale netting on this lure simply because I wanted you to see that nice lures can be made with or without scales.

**Try surface lures in early morning and the calm before a storm.**

# LURE 6
# Pan Fish

Let's make a lure for pan fish—fish that are small enough to fit in a pan, but big enough to be legal. Bass and pike are lots of fun, but you can't beat pan fish, such as blue gills, crappies, or perch, on an ultralight rod and reel. My favorite saying is, "It's a good thing God never made a six-pound blue-gill, because you'd never land him!" This lure is a minnow type that has a propeller at the front and sinks, painted in general minnow coloration—another **scrap wood** and **airbrush** job.

# Pan Fish Pattern

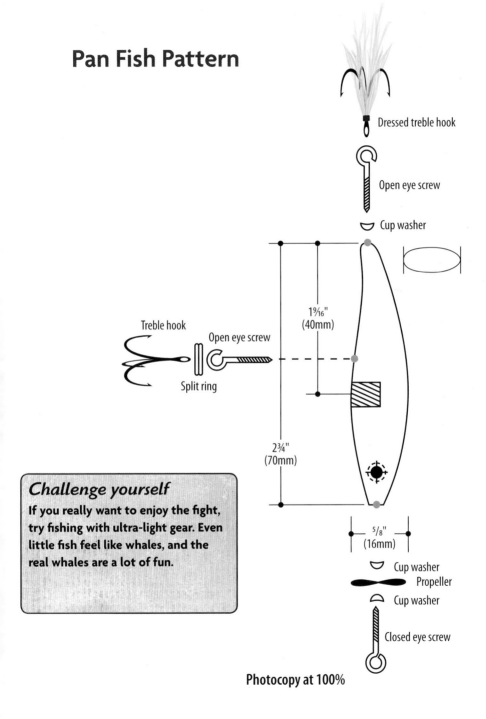

Dressed treble hook

Open eye screw

Cup washer

Treble hook

Open eye screw

Split ring

1⁹⁄₁₆"
(40mm)

2¾"
(70mm)

⁵⁄₈"
(16mm)

Cup washer
Propeller
Cup washer

Closed eye screw

**Challenge yourself**
If you really want to enjoy the fight, try fishing with ultra-light gear. Even little fish feel like whales, and the real whales are a lot of fun.

**Photocopy at 100%**

# Materials and tools list

## Materials
- 1 by 4 scrap wood
- Solid brass beads (counter weights)
- 3-D lure eyes

## Hardware
### Front assembly:
- Closed eye screw
- 2 cup washers
- Propeller

### Belly assembly:
- Open eye screw
- Treble hook
- Split ring

### Rear assembly:
- Open eye screw
- Cup washer
- Dressed treble hook (See page 163)

## Tools
- Band saw
- Pencil
- Handheld power drill
- Drill bit to match counter weight beads
- ¹⁄₁₆" (2mm)-diameter twist drill bit
- 5-minute epoxy
- Coarse foam fingernail board
- Knife (optional)

- Small mesh scale netting
- Rag
- Toothpick
- Prick punch
- Fine point black permanent marker

## Painting supplies
- Flat white base coat spray
- Airbrush
- Acetone
- Lacquer paints: metallic silver, transparent light green, black umber, gill red
- Cardboard
- Clear spray finish

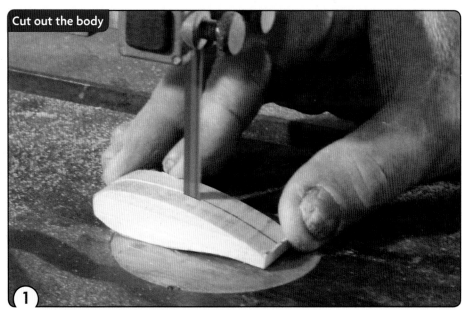

**Cut out the body**

① Cut the lure out of some 1 by 4 scrap wood. Because this lure is so small, we will rip it down the middle and make two lures, each about ³⁄₈" (10mm) wide. When you are cutting this little lure down the middle, be really careful and watch those fingers. Remember to lower the blade guard to the proper place—it's raised in this photo so you can see the blade position.

## Install counter weights

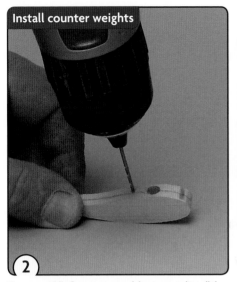

**2**

Use your middle finger gauge and draw a centerline all the way around the lure. Drill the weight hole using a bit that matches the beads and the belly hook pilot hole with a 1/16" (2mm) twist bit. Go ahead and drill the nose and tail pilot holes as well. Remember to secure the lure in a bench vise if you don't feel comfortable holding it by hand.

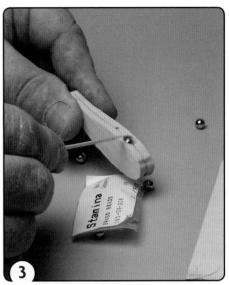

**3**

Because lead is no longer an option, we will be using solid brass beads for the weights. As with all weights, glue them in with epoxy and leave a dome so you can finish-sand it flush to the belly with a coarse foam fingernail board.

## Dry-fit hardware

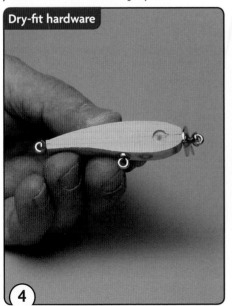

**4**

Now is the time to dry-fit all of the hardware, including the nose propeller. Notice the eyeholes. You can locate and drill these at any time prior to painting with the base coat/primer.

## Shape and basecoat

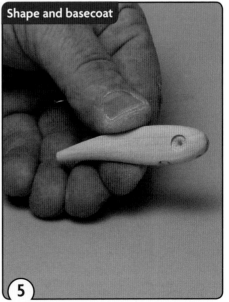

**5**

The lure is so small that a knife or fingernail board is the easiest and safest way to shape the minnow body. Of course, you will need to sand the shape smooth and re-drill the eyeholes if necessary.

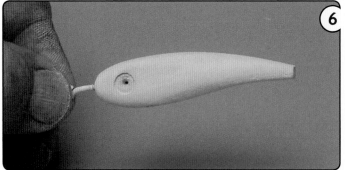

**6** Insert the painting handle into the front of the lure. Give the minnow a couple of coats of the flat white base coat. Let it dry overnight and then lightly sand and wipe as we have done before.

**7** We are going to paint this lure in a natural minnow color scheme. Load the airbrush with metallic silver and acetone. Paint the upper two-thirds of the body, leaving a white stripe down the belly. You want an even, but light, coat of the silver.

**Paint scales**

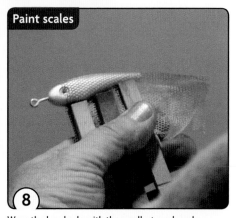

**8** Wrap the lure body with the smallest mesh scale netting that you have. Notice that the netting starts at the middle of the eye and continues to the tail. There are no scales on the head.

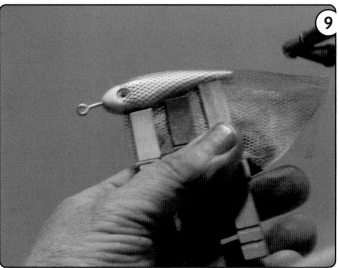

**9** Mix a batch of the transparent light green and paint over the previous coat of silver. Our past projects used gold as the base color coat; here you can see how much lighter the green looks with silver under it. That is exactly what we are after.

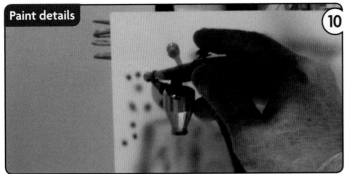

**Paint details**

**10** Next we mix up a batch of black umber, but this time only fill the cup one-quarter full and complete the fill-up with acetone. This gives us a 1:3 ratio. Adjust your spray fan to as fine a line as you can get. Check the setting on the cardboard.

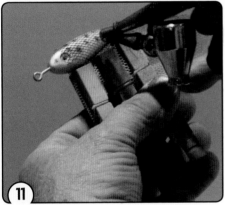

**11** Paint random small spots on the upper half of the body, including the head. Do not paint spots below the lateral line.

## Painting spots

Whenever you paint spots, always have a rag handy and use it after every seven or ten spots. The low air pressure allows paint to build up at the tip, and if you don't occasionally wipe it off, it will eventually spit all over your paint job. I don't think you really want to start all over again!

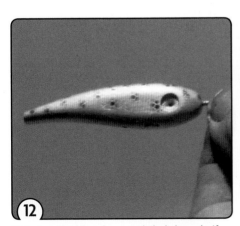

**12** Notice how the colors change with the light angle. If you do not like the look of the scales in the spots, just take the netting off before you do the spotting.

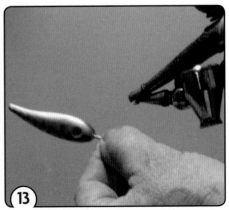

**13** Mix up a small batch of gill red and paint a small spot where the throat latch would be. You want a lot of contrast here, so give the throat latch two or three coats of red.

**Try light or metallic finish on surface lures for clear water.**

**Apply finishing touches**

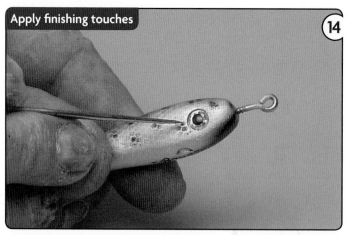

**14** Mix some 5-minute epoxy and put a small drop in the center of each eyehole. Use your prick punch to install the 3-D eyes.

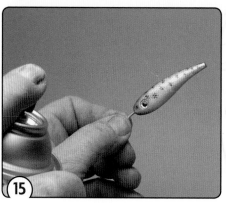

**15** Use your fine point permanent marker to sign your lure. Make sure to seal the ink with a couple of puff coats of the clear and then wait 30 minutes or so. Give the entire lure three light coats of clear at 20-minute intervals, and hang it up to cure for 24 hours.

**Install hardware**

**16** As with all of the lures, arrange the hardware exactly as it will go onto the lure. Assemble the hardware, and we are done.

**17** Here is our finished pan fish minnow—an uncommonly handsome little fellow.

# Minnow Chaser

This is a lure I came up with as a way to add attraction to the minnow lure type. This is a 4½" (114mm) **scrap wood** minnow body that sinks and has a spinner attached at the nose. The entire purpose of the spinner is to make it appear your lure is chasing a bait fish. That is why I call the whole lure a chaser. This lure has proven to be very effective on bass, pike, and salmon, both retrieved and trolled. This is a fun project and another chance to practice your **airbrushing** skills.

# Minnow Chaser Pattern

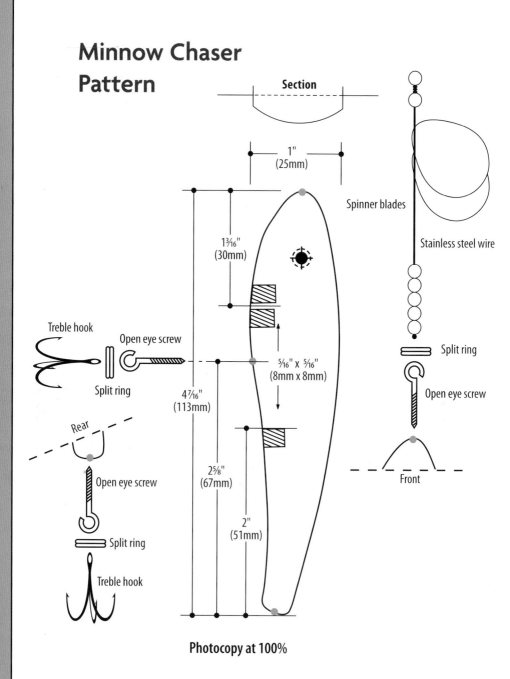

Section

1"
(25mm)

1³⁄₁₆"
(30mm)

Spinner blades

Stainless steel wire

Treble hook

Open eye screw

Split ring

Split ring

Open eye screw

5⁄₁₆" x 5⁄₁₆"
(8mm x 8mm)

Front

4⁷⁄₁₆"
(113mm)

Rear

Open eye screw

Split ring

Treble hook

2⁵⁄₈"
(67mm)

2"
(51mm)

**Photocopy at 100%**

# Materials and tools list

## Materials
- 4½" (114mm) long, ¾" (19mm)-thick wood
- Brass spinner bodies, brass beads (belly weights)
- Flat lure eyes

### Front assembly:
- Stainless steel wire (.028" to .035" diameter)
- 2 spinner blades of your choice
- 2 clevises
- Spinner beads—hollow for retrieving, solid for trolling
- Orange salmon egg bead
- Open eye screw
- Cup washer

## Belly assembly:
- Open eye screw
- Split ring
- Treble hook

## Rear assembly:
- Open eye screw
- Split ring
- Treble hook

## Tools
- Band saw
- Pencil
- Ruler
- Handheld power drill
- ¼" (6mm) brad-point drill bit
- 5-minute epoxy

- Small tack hammer
- Wire-forming or round nose pliers
- Fine mesh scale netting
- Prick punch
- Fine point black permanent marker

## Painting supplies
- Flat white spray paint
- Damp cloth
- Airbrush
- Acetone
- Lacquer paints: metallic silver, transparent green light, black umber, gill red, cover white
- Clear spray finish

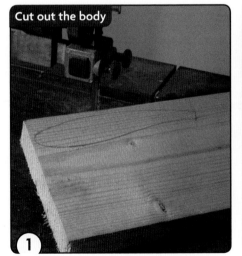

**Cut out the body**

**1** This 4 ½" (114mm) minnow starts out like all the rest—with a scrap of ¾" (19mm)-thick wood. If all you have is a 2 by 4 and the like, that will work just fine; simply rip it into more bodies. Using the pattern, trace the outline onto the board. Orient the wood grain to run the length of the lure from head to tail.

**2** Cut out the lure body. I start by making the cut at the tail, then cut the back and belly from the head to the tail. This saves you from wasting good wood for the saw blade run-out. Remember to lower the blade guard to the proper place—it's raised in this photo so you can see the blade position.

**3** We only need a ½" (13mm)-thick body, so use the middle finger method (see page 93) to draw a line around the lure. Make the rip cut. Be very careful getting this close to any cutting blade, because they don't care what they cut.

**Lay out centerlines**

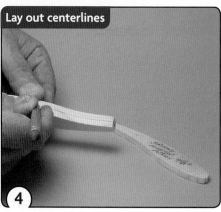

**4** Use the middle finger method again to draw a line all the way around the minnow. This time, the line will be in the center. The ¼" (6mm) slab is in the background, cleaned up a bit and marked as a template.

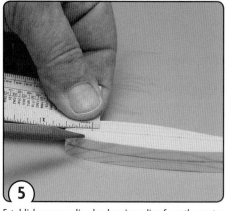

**5** Establish your eye line by drawing a line from the center of the nose to the center of the tail. Measure from the nose along the eye line to locate the center of the eye, or transfer the location from the pattern.

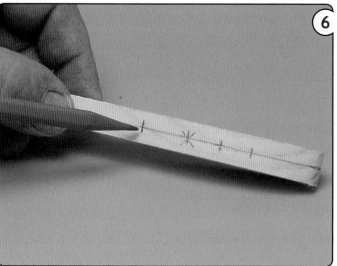

**6** Measure and mark the weight and hook hole locations along the belly line. Notice one location is marked by an X, so you can remember which is the hook pilot hole.

**Drill pilot holes**

**7** Drill out the three weight holes with a ¼" (6mm) brad-point drill bit. Remember to secure the lure in a bench vise if you don't feel comfortable holding it by hand.

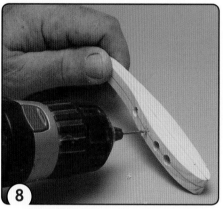

**8** Change bits to the ¹⁄₁₆" (2mm) pilot drill bit and drill the belly hook location.

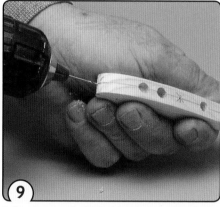

**9** Drill in the nose pilot hole. Make sure you run in the drill bit parallel with all of the centerlines—in other words, make it go straight in. Finish by drilling in the tail hook location too. Switch to a bit sized to fit the eyeholes and drill those as well.

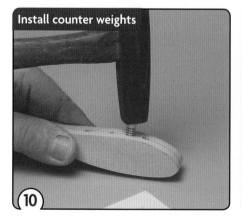

**Install counter weights**

**10** Here we are going to install the belly weights. I'm using brass spinner bodies. Put some five-minute epoxy in the bottom of the weight hole. Use a small tack hammer to drive the weights home.

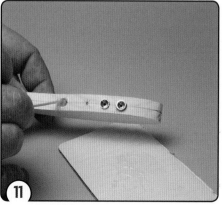

**11** The most rearward hole is quite shallow, so I'm gluing in a brass bead at that location instead. As with all weight gluing, make sure to leave a hump of glue on top of the bead. Sand the weights and glue flush to the belly.

fishy fact

"A bad day of fishing is better than a good day of work."

**Dry-fit hardware**

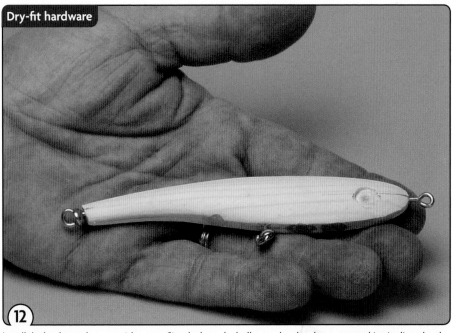

**12**

Install the hardware that you wish to use. Give the lure a look all around and make sure everything is aligned and looking good. Remove the hardware and set it aside.

**Apply basecoat**

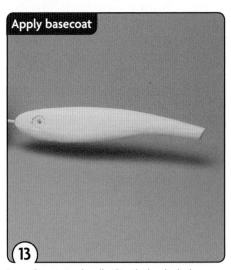

**13**

Insert the painting handle. Give the lure body the usual two to three coats of flat white base coat. Please remember: 20 minutes between coats, wait overnight to cure, lightly sand, and wipe with a damp cloth.

**Make chaser**

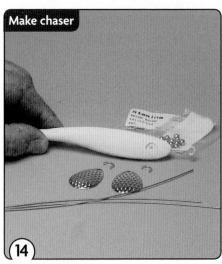

**14**

We will take this opportunity to make the chaser. You will need some stainless steel wire (.028" to .035" diameter), two spinner blades of your choice, two clevises, and some spinner beads.

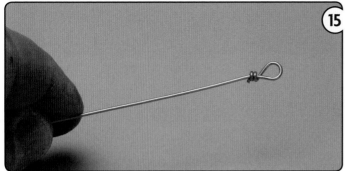

**15** Use the wire-forming pliers to form a loop at one end of the wire. I usually wrap three turns around, but you only need one complete wrap to ensure strength. You can purchase wires like this from lure parts suppliers with an eye already formed, too.

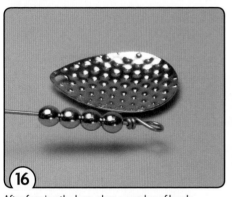

**16** After forming the loop, place a number of beads onto the wire to equal the length of the blades. For a retrieving type lure use hollow beads (to keep weight down) but for trolling types use the solid beads (to get the weight up).

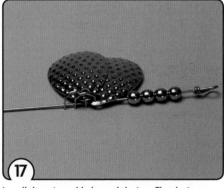

**17** Install the spinner blades and clevises. The clevis allows a spinner blade to rotate around the wire. I like to interlock the clevises (as shown), but they can be equally effective when stacked. If you opt to separate the blades, be sure to put an additional bead between them to ensure they are free spinning.

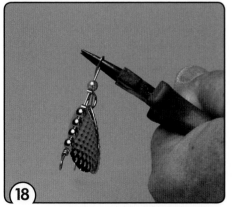

**18** Add one orange bead above the clevises. Grab the wire ¼" (6mm) above the bead with your pliers and bend the free end around the pliers until it is 90° to the chaser.

## Spinner orientation

When building any type of spinner, make sure you have the blades in the proper orientation. This means the cupped face of the blade goes against the wire and the pointy end goes to the front. This chaser is being built tail to nose, so check the blade orientation in this photograph.

Try white or silver prop blades in clear water.

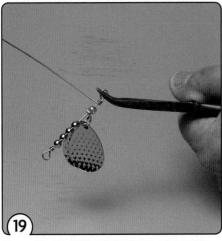

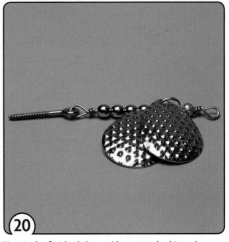

**19**

**20**

After making the 90° bend, simply wrap the straight end around the chaser, thus forming a finishing loop. Make sure that the finish wrap does not go right against the bead, or the spinner will not turn freely. Leave ¹⁄₁₆" to ⅛" (2mm to 3mm) of clearance.

Here is the finished chaser. I have attached it to the front eye screw. It goes without saying that colors and shapes of the blades and beads are infinitely variable, so feel free to make the chasers in any combination your local fish like.

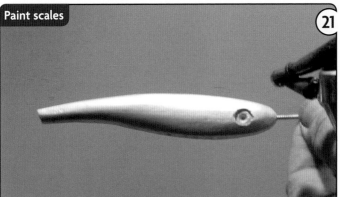

**Paint scales**

**21**

We are going to paint the lure to look like a rainbow trout. Start with the usual mix/back flush of metallic silver. Give the upper two-thirds of the body a good even coat of the silver. Make sure you are leaving a white belly.

**22**

Load up and mix a batch of transparent green light. Wrap the lure with fine mesh scale netting and secure with your modified clothespins. Notice the netting starts just behind the eyehole. Apply a light coat of green to the sides and back.

**23** Start at the back and apply a second light coat down as far as the eye line—not as far down as the first coat.

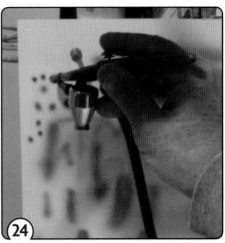

**24** Mix a small batch of black umber at a paint-to-thinner ratio of 1:3. When painting very fine detail, you want to have exceptionally thin paint so the airbrush will work well at minimum air pressure and paint flow. Set the spray fan to a very light line and test it.

## Adjusting paint flow

An airbrush is adjustable as to paint flow and air pressure, but you can also make lines finer or wider by how close you hold the gun to the surface. Close is narrower and father away is wider.

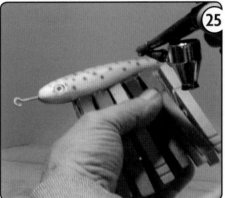

**25** Start spotting the back of the trout as randomly (both location and size) as you can manage. Rainbow trout have no spots below their lateral line, so be aware of that before you go spot-crazy. Give the spots a second coat to darken them. Remember to wipe the tip every few spots to prevent splatters.

**Paint details**

**26** Remove the scale netting for the rest of the paint job. Load and mix a standard batch of gill red. Set the brush to a very fine line, and make sure to test it. Lightly shade-in the cheeks (gill covers) just behind the eye. This is a defining characteristic of rainbow trout.

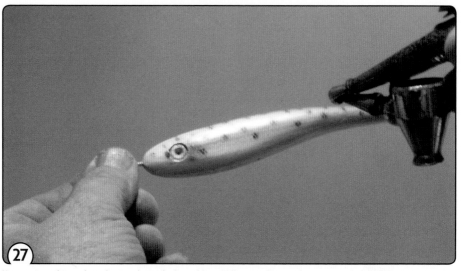

27

Next, paint a thin, pale-red stripe down the lateral line. Make sure the initial pass is very light, because you can always make it more vivid with subsequent coats. The vividness of the red stripe is purely personal, because rainbow trouts' stripes can vary from nearly invisible to scarlet.

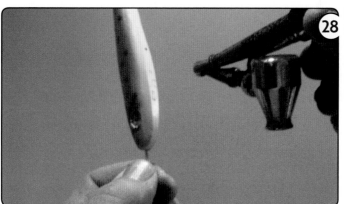

28 Mix up a small batch of cover white to our regular 1:2 ratio. Paint in a very bright, but narrow, white stripe down the middle of the belly.

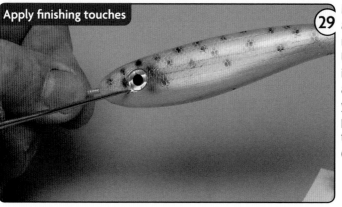

**Apply finishing touches**

29 Mix some 5-minute epoxy and put a small drop in the middle of each eyehole. Use your prick punch to install the eyes. Notice we are using flat eyes—after you set the eyes, use the punch handle to flatten the eye tight to the bottom of the eyehole.

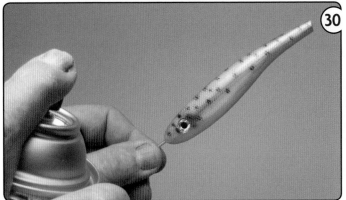

**30** Let 'em know who made it. Make sure to seal your signature with a couple of puff coats of clear. Remember to let it set for about 20 minutes. Give this puppy two to three coats of clear spray, 20 minutes apart, and let it cure for 24 hours.

### Install hardware

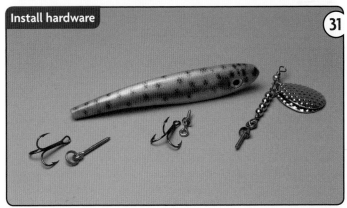

**31** Assemble your hardware and lay it out exactly the way you will install it. Now install the hardware and please remember to seal the screws with a little glue.

**32** How could any self-respecting predator resist this? Heck, I just might attack it!

# LURE 8
# Floating-Diving Frog

Our next lure is a floating-diving frog bass bait. The frog painting scheme is a true classic and I thought you might like to make one of these. Generally, frog lures are made as surface baits only, while ours will be a surface lure that is able to dive if we want it to. You'll need a **purchased popper blank** and your **airbrush.**

# Floating-Diving Frog Pattern

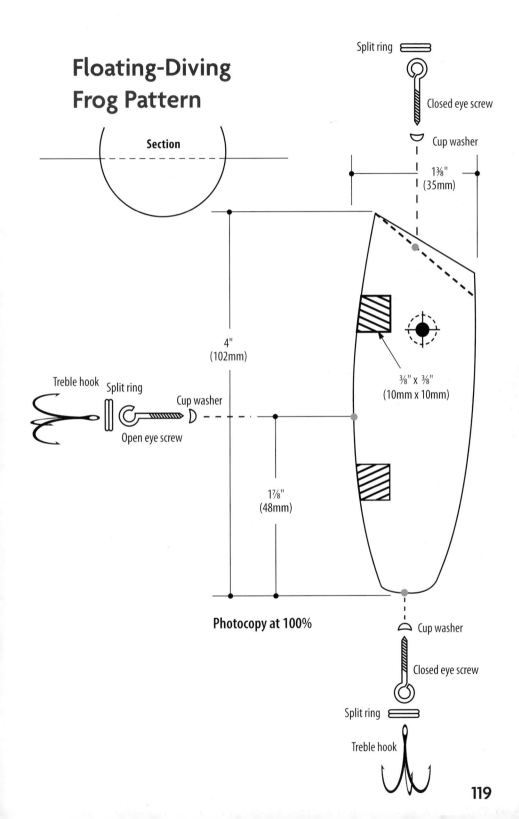

**Section**

Split ring

Closed eye screw

Cup washer

1⅜"
(35mm)

⅜" x ⅜"
(10mm x 10mm)

4"
(102mm)

Treble hook   Split ring

Cup washer

Open eye screw

1⅞"
(48mm)

**Photocopy at 100%**

Cup washer

Closed eye screw

Split ring

Treble hook

**119**

# Materials and tools list

## Materials
- Purchased popper blank
- Solid brass beads (counter weights)
- 3-D lure eyes

## Hardware
**Front assembly:**
- Closed eye screw
- Split ring
- Cup washer

**Belly assembly:**
- Open eye screw
- Cup washer
- Treble hook

## Rear assembly:
- Closed eye screw
- Cup washer
- Split ring
- Treble hook

## Tools
- Pencil
- Flexible ruler
- Handheld power drill
- ¹⁄₁₆" (2mm) twist drill bit
- Drill bit to match eye size
- Drill bit to match counter weights
- 5-minute epoxy
- Coarse foam fingernail board

- Rag
- Toothpick
- Prick punch
- Fine point black permanent marker

## Painting supplies
- Flat white base coat spray
- Airbrush
- Acetone
- Lacquer paints: glimmer gold, transparent light green, medium green, medium yellow, black umber, cover white
- Cardboard
- Clear spray finish

### Modify the body

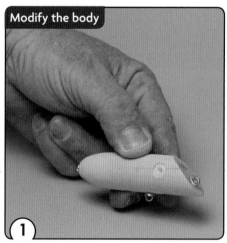

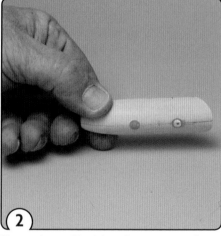

**1** We are going to start with a purchased popper blank and invert it. The intended belly becomes the back. Draw in the centerlines and eye lines. It's also a good time to measure and drill your eye and pilot holes. Dry-fit your hardware, making sure everything lines up properly.

**2** We are going to add weight so that we can use a fast retrieve and maintain a good posture. Drill a couple of shallow weight holes fore and aft of the belly hook pilot hole and insert a solid brass bead in each; cover with 5-minute epoxy. Use your coarse foam fingernail board to sand the epoxy flush with the belly.

**Apply basecoats**

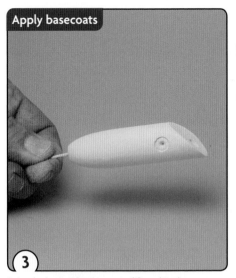

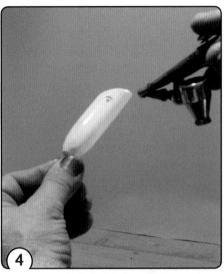

Paint the lure with two coats of flat white base coat spray. Make sure you cure it overnight, lightly sand it, and wipe with a damp rag before you start painting.

We will start our frog paint scheme by laying down a color base coat of glimmer gold, so go ahead and mix a batch at the standard ratio of 1:2, and mix with the back-flush method. Lay on two coats of the gold to the upper two-thirds of the lure, including the face.

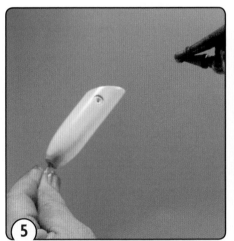

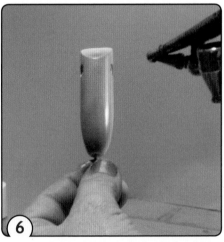

We will need a batch of the transparent light green next. Go ahead and mix that to the standard ratio. Paint over the gold with the light green. We are looking for a chartreuse color, just about like that in this photograph.

Next, you will want to mix a regular batch of medium green. Use the medium green to paint the back (upper third) of the lure body. A couple of light coats will do. Notice the face in this photo—you can see that the medium green does not cover all of the chartreuse.

fishy fact

**Structure: Feature on the water bottom; drop-off, sandbar.**

**Paint spots**

**7**

The next color will be medium yellow, mixed to the standard ratio. Clean the gun thoroughly before mixing. Set for a fine line. Spray yellow spots randomly, changing size and shape. Mix up the shapes for more authenticity. The exact shade of the spots is up to you.

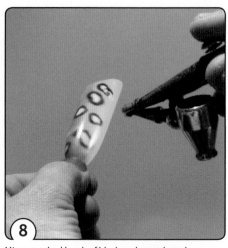

**8**

Mix a standard batch of black umber and set the spray fan for as fine a line as you can. Make sure to test the setting on your cardboard. Use the black to paint a border around each yellow spot. This photo shows just how irregular the spots really are.

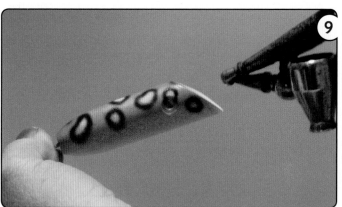

**9**

I usually give the spot halos a second coat to make them nice and dark, the reason being that I like a lot of contrast. If you like the way the halos look after one coat, then stop at that point. Again, this is one of those personal taste things, so use your own judgment.

**Apply details**

**10**

Our next color will be cover white, so clean your airbrush out. The white should be the regular 1:2 ratio. Paint the belly to a nice bright white. If you have ever picked up a leopard frog, you know their bellies are nearly snow white.

**11** Mix up some 5-minute epoxy and use a toothpick to put a drop in each eyehole. Use the prick punch to set in a pair of gold 3-D eyes. Don't forget your signature. Set the ink with our regular two puff coats of clear finish.

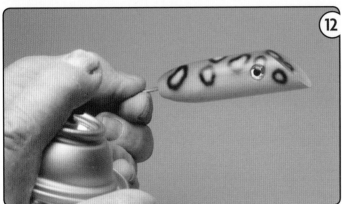

**12** The lure is going to need its two to three clear coats. You know the routine: light coats 20 minutes apart and 24 hours to cure. You are probably getting sick of hearing it, but please keep the finish coats light. They cure faster and give a lot better overall results.

**Install hardware**

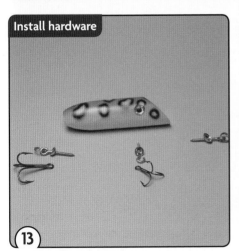

**13** As usual, lay out your hardware exactly as it will go on the lure before you install anything. When you are satisfied, put a drop of glue in the pilot holes and run the mounting screws in snug.

**14** Here's our completed frog. I'm sure that somewhere, at a bass cafeteria, he's on the entrée menu.

fishy fact

Cover: Natural or manmade fish hide-out; grass, rock, pilings.

123

# LURE 9
# Sinking Wiggler

This Sinking Wiggler attracts bass and pike by doing just what is says—sinking and wiggling. The design is essentially a minnow lure with the head cut off on an angle. I designed this to **scrapwood** lure fish when the bass and Northerns are suspended, meaning in 5' to 10' (1½m to 3m) of water. We are going to paint this guy in a fire-tiger perch fingerling scheme using our **airbrush**. This is a fun project and a really effective lure as well.

# Sinking Wiggler Pattern

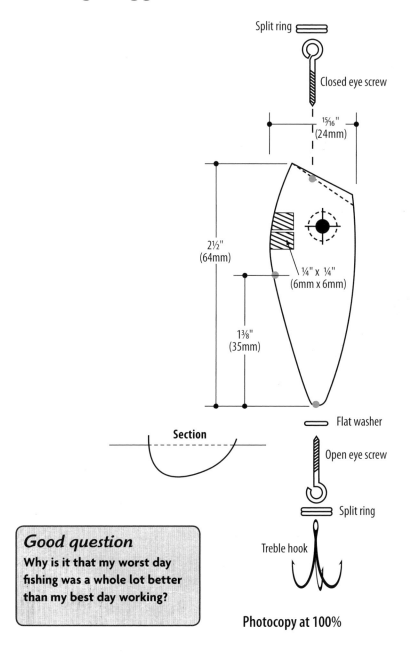

Split ring

Closed eye screw

$^{15}/_{16}$" (24mm)

$2\frac{1}{2}$" (64mm)

$\frac{1}{4}$" x $\frac{1}{4}$" (6mm x 6mm)

$1\frac{3}{8}$" (35mm)

**Section**

Flat washer

Open eye screw

Split ring

Treble hook

Photocopy at 100%

*Good question*
**Why is it that my worst day fishing was a whole lot better than my best day working?**

125

## Materials and tools list

### Materials
- ¾" (19mm)-thick scrap
- Brass spinner bodies (counter weights)
- 3-D lure eyes

### Hardware
**Front assembly:**
- Closed eye screw
- Split ring

**Rear assembly:**
- Open eye screw
- Flat washer
- Split ring
- Treble hook

### Tools
- Band saw
- Pencil
- Flexible ruler
- Handheld power drill
- Drill bit sized to fit counter weights
- ¹⁄₁₆" (2mm) twist drill bit
- Drill bit sized to fit eyes
- Five-minute epoxy
- Tack hammer
- Toothpick
- Coarse fingernail board
- Sink partially filled with water
- Prick punch
- Fine point black permanent marker

### Painting supplies
- Flat white base spray
- Airbrush
- Acetone
- Lacquer paints: glimmer gold, transparent green light, medium green, medium yellow, gill red, black umber
- Clear spray finish

**Shape and add weight**

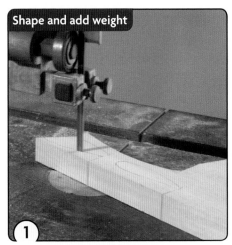

**1** We start this lure with some ¾" (19mm)-thick scrap. I always start sawing by making a tail cut. I then cut from the head toward the tail on both the back and the belly. This preserves more of the board for the next lure. Remember to lower the blade guard to the proper place—it's raised in this photo so you can see the blade position.

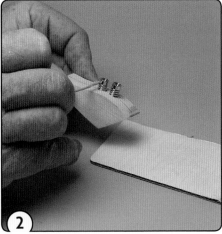

**2** Draw in your centerlines and mark two weight holes on the belly centerline as per the pattern recommendations. Use a drill bit sized to fit the brass spinner bodies and drill the holes. Dry-fit the weights first, then set them with some 5-minute epoxy.

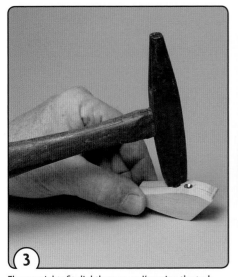

(3)

These weights fit slightly snug, so I'm using the tack hammer to set them with light taps. When they are flush with the belly, fill in the holes with the epoxy. Use a toothpick to work the epoxy into the small nooks and crannies. Sand the weights flush using the coarse fingernail board.

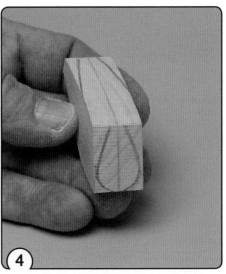

(4)

Using the photos of the finished piece, mark out the lure's profile so we can make it round. Remember that centerlines are pretty easy to draw when using the middle finger method. In this example, the face is flat, but it can also be cupped. In either case the lure will wiggle.

**Dry-fit and float test**

(5)

After making the lure round and drilling the pilot and eyeholes, dry-fit the hardware and give him the eyeball test.

(6)

The next step is the old sink test. I always do this on a sinking lure, mostly because I don't want to brag-up my new sinking lure, only to find out it floats. Toss the lure in a sink full of water—if the thing floats, there is a slight chance it may not work as expected!

**Apply basecoats**

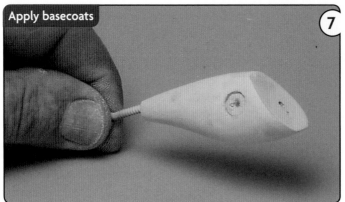

**7** The next step is the flat white basecoat. I guess by now you have this whole process down pat!

**8** Our fire tiger paint scheme starts with a base color coat of glimmer gold. As usual, use the 1:2 ratio. Paint the entire lure (except a thin belly stripe of white) with two coats of the gold paint. Remember, the belly is on the side where the body is longest.

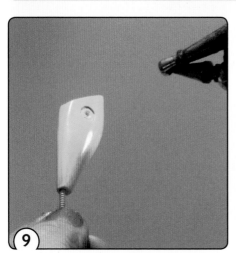

**9** Our next color will be transparent green light. Mix this batch with the usual 1:2 ratio of paint to acetone. Apply the green on top of the gold to obtain a medium chartreuse color. This photo shows the approximate color we are looking for.

**Paint back and belly**

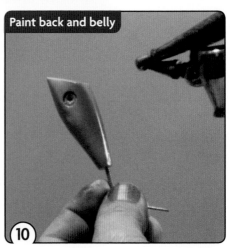

**10** Our third color will be a standard mix of medium green. Paint the back and sides, but only down to the eye line. Make sure to also darken the top of the face.

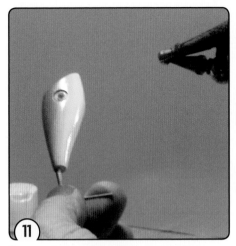

**11** Our next color is medium yellow; yes, make the standard ratio. This color is lighter than the previous one, so guess what? Clean that airbrush. Paint the belly and lower sides. We are not looking for a solid yellow; we want yellowish chartreuse.

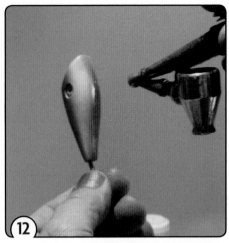

**12** Our next-to-final color will be gill red in our standard mix. Set the airbrush fan to a fine line and paint the center of the belly. Notice that after two to three coats, the belly looks dark orange. However, if you prefer a deep red color, then one to two additional coats will do it.

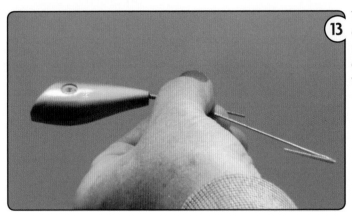

**13** This angle shows the color contrast of what commercial makers call fire tiger and gives you a fair idea of what we are after.

**Apply details**

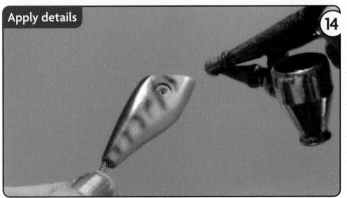

**14** Mix a small standard batch of black umber and rough in the center of the back and the side stripes. Make the side stripes wavy. Why? The real reason is they look darned good! Re-coat as necessary until the shade of black suits your taste as to contrast. Usually, two to three coats give excellent results.

fishy fact — Thermocline: Where rising warm water and sinking cold water meet.

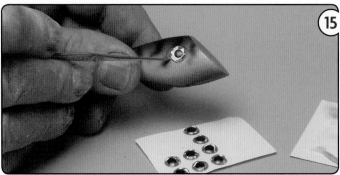

**15** Mix up some 5-minute epoxy and put a small drop into the center of each eyehole. Use the prick punch to set your 3-D eyes. I prefer gold eyes for this paint scheme.

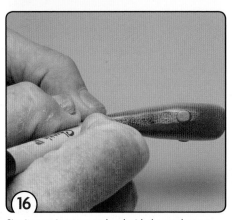

**16** Give it your signature, and seal with the regular two puff coats of clear. As with all our lures, give it two to three clear coats, 20 minutes apart, and let the whole thing cure for 24 hours.

**Install hardware**

**17** Lay out the necessary hardware. Put a touch of glue in the pilot holes and run the screws down snug. On this style of lure, I commonly use a flat washer at the tail hook to serve as a wear plate. This allows me to change eye screws without undue damage to the lure body.

**18** Behold! Our fire-tiger perch fingerling in all its glory.

# Mallard Duckling

This project involves carving a duck, albeit a baby duck. No, I have not gone completely around the bend. This springtime lure is perfect for two massive predators: pike and musky. Since I live up North, I usually make these to resemble a mallard. It would also be effective as an in-shore saltwater lure near mangrove areas where shore birds nest. This project is fairly lengthy, but like most things, it takes longer to explain than to do. If your patience allows, the end results are well worth it. You'll need some **scrap wood** and your **acrylics and brushes**!

# Mallard Duckling Pattern

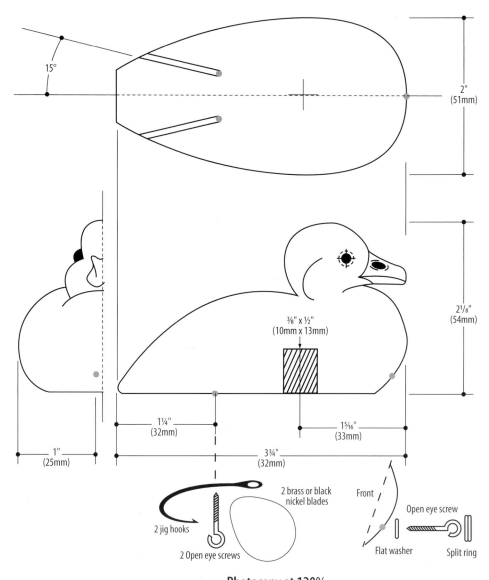

15°

2"
(51mm)

2¹⁄₈"
(54mm)

³⁄₈" x ¹⁄₂"
(10mm x 13mm)

1¹⁄₄"
(32mm)

1⁵⁄₁₆"
(33mm)

1"
(25mm)

3³⁄₄"
(32mm)

2 jig hooks

2 Open eye screws

2 brass or black
nickel blades

Front

Open eye screw

Flat washer

Split ring

Photocopy at 120%

# Materials and tools list

## Materials
- Tupelo or piece of 4 by 4
- Brass spinner body (counter weight)
- 3-D lure eyes or glass taxidermy eyes

## Hardware
### Front assembly:
- Open eye screw
- Flat washer
- Split ring

### Belly assembly:
- 2 jig hooks, ¼ oz.
- 2 open eye screws
- 2 brass or black nickel blades

## Tools
- Band saw
- Pencil
- Masking tape
- Flexible ruler
- Power carving tool
- Sanding drum for power carver or knife and sanding stick
- Fine ruby power carving bit
- Assorted grit sandpaper
- Handheld power drill
- ⅜" (10mm) brad-point drill bit
- 1⁄16" (2mm) twist drill bit
- Drill bit to match size of eyes
- 5-minute epoxy
- Tack hammer
- Side-cutters
- Chisel
- Utility knife
- Hacksaw blade
- Woodburner
- Old toothbrush
- Apoxie Sculpt
- Toothpick
- Sink filled with water
- Paper towel

## Painting supplies
- Gesso or flat white spray
- Acrylic paints: yellow oxide, raw sienna, burnt sienna, black
- Flat fan brush
- Size 0 script liner
- Hair dryer
- Clear fingernail polish
- Clear gloss or matte spray

---

**Cut out the body**

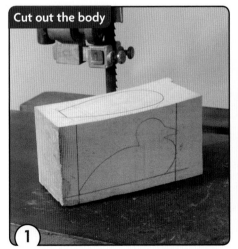

**1**

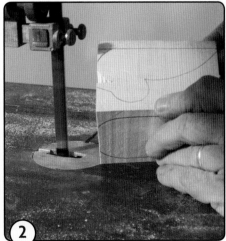

**2**

Lay out the duckling pattern on a suitably sized piece of scrap wood. In this case, I'm using a piece of tupelo, but any piece of 4 by 4 will do. Notice that I have simply drawn in the end lines.

Before we actually start on the lure, cut off those end lines. Make your first cuts where the bill and breast meet. Discard the waste. Next, cut off the bottom of the block (belly line). Save the scrap piece.

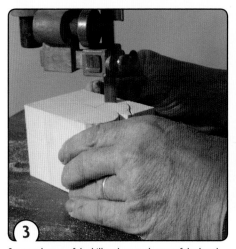

**3** Start at the top of the bill and cut to the top of the head, then stop. Turn the block around and cut from the tail to where you stopped the previous cut. This will leave the top piece intact. Save this piece. These two cuts don't follow the exact outline. Go back and trim out the details.

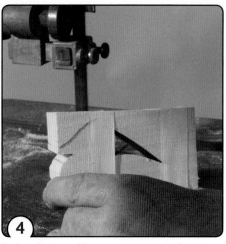

**4** Replace the top and bottom waste pieces and secure them with masking tape. I do this because I can now cut out the top view and be sure all of the cuts are square and correct.

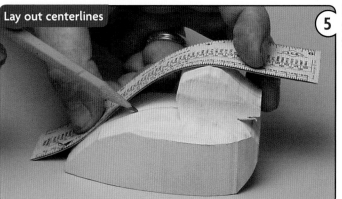

Lay out centerlines

**5** Use the flexible plastic ruler to draw in a centerline all the way around the body: back, belly, head, and bill.

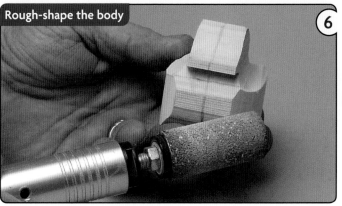

Rough-shape the body

**6** Start the shaping by narrowing the width of the head. I'm using a power carving tool here, but you can as easily use a knife and round sanding stick if you desire. This photo shows what we are going for at this stage. Remember to secure the lure in a bench vise if you don't feel comfortable holding it by hand.

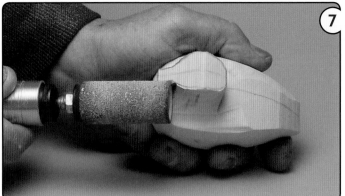

**7** Use a pencil to lay out a rough shape on top of the head. Carve the head to shape.

**8** When you have the head roughed in, start rounding off the corners on the body. Don't forget to round off the belly line as well. This is the look we want after roughing in with the coarse tools.

### Refine the shape

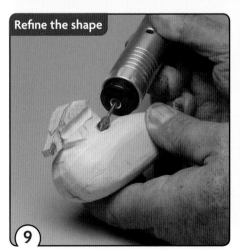

**9** Here I have changed carving bits to a fine ruby carver. Start refining the head shape by cutting in the eye lines. Carve in the front of the cheek and the rear of the head/body line. This photo gives you a fair idea of what we want to accomplish at this point.

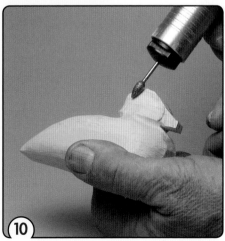

**10** Now start to round the head. Keep in mind that the head has two parts. There is the part from the eye line and upwards, and the area from the eye line to the body.

fishy fact

**Try fishing at night during the summer.**

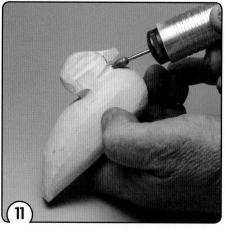

**11** Our next step is to round the body into the head and neck. Notice the top of the head above the eye line.

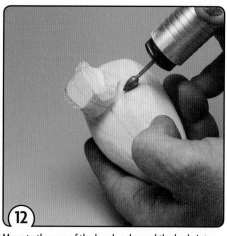

**12** Move to the rear of the head and round the body into that area as well.

## Mark hardware locations

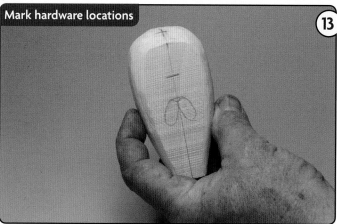

**13** At this point, I have marked the belly for the counter weight and the two jig hooks we will be using. You can also see the line tie location on the lower breast area (top of the photo).

## Define wings and beak

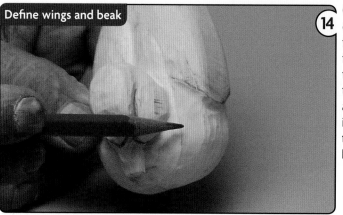

**14** Go back to the carver and cut in a line to define the front of the wings. Cut in this line, and then round the breast area so it is lower than the wing. While you are at it, make a depression in the middle of the back to make a separation line between the wings.

**15** Now use the pointed end of the carving bit to work in the contours of the bill.

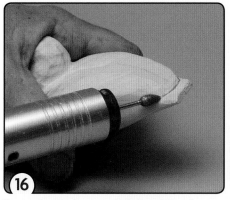

**16** Next, cut in a line between the body and the tail feathers. Then carve the tail feather wood down so it is below the height of the body feathers.

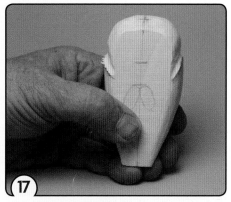

**17** Check the belly hardware locations. As you work the wing lines down into the belly, this will make it easier to create symmetrical parts and avoid any conflicts between wood and metal.

## Smooth the body

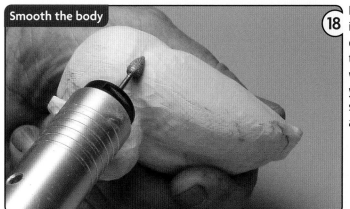

**18** Next, smooth the wings into the body. Ducklings are covered in pin feathers, so they tend to look fuzzy. Your work will go a lot better if you constantly think "round, soft, and fuzzy" while you are carving.

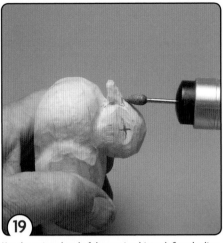

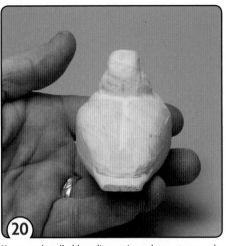

**19** Use the pointed end of the carving bit to define the line where the bill and head meet.

**20** Use some handheld medium-grit sandpaper to smooth and soften the body profile. I usually start this process at the belly and work up. Fine-sand the head and cheeks. This softening will show you any asymmetry that needs correcting.

## Keep perspective

By jumping back-and-forth between different areas of the duckling's body, you are forced to look the whole thing over. This is a good technique for keeping the entire shape in perspective as you concentrate on the details.

**Prepare the jig hooks**

**21** Use a ⅜" (10mm) brad-point drill bit to start excavating the jig head holes. Notice that by drilling a series of holes it is very easy to cut in the slots.

**22** Set the counter weight with 5-minute epoxy and a tack hammer. Use your side-cutters to snip off the hook eyes on the jig heads.

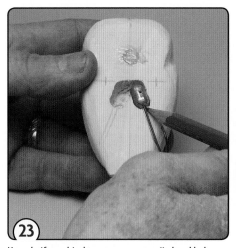

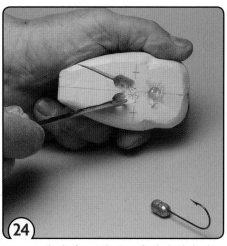

**(23)** Use a knife or chisel to square-up your jig head holes. Lay in the jig heads and mark the hook shanks.

**(24)** Use your utility knife to make V cuts for the hook shanks. Use a handheld hacksaw blade to saw in the precise slots. It is very easy to control the depth this way.

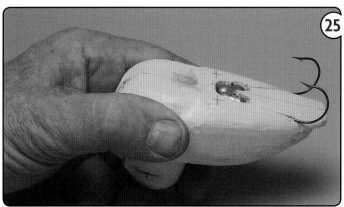

**(25)** The jig hooks are inset to the proper depth—just below the surface. Notice the two X marks even with the hook weights? These are the pilot holes for the flip feet.

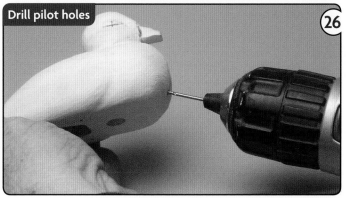

Drill pilot holes

**(26)** After sanding the belly smooth, drill in the three remaining pilot holes. This photograph shows the angle I use for the line-tie screw pilot hole.

fishy fact

**Tread lightly when wading in to avoid spooking fish.**

## Create feather flow

(27)

Hand sand the entire bird with fine sandpaper until it's all soft and fuzzy. Pencil in feather flow lines. It is a whole lot easier to erase a pencil line than it is to throw away your burned-in mistakes. I am not prepared to say how many I have actually thrown away, but I recommend drawing those lines first.

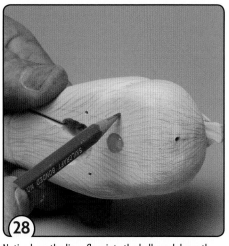

(28)

Notice how the lines flow into the belly and down the breast. At this point, we need to dry-fit the mounting screws. Now is also the time to drill in the eyeholes, using a drill bit to match the size of the eyes.

### Curving pyrography

When you need to curve the lines, simply roll the burner pen with your thumb and forefinger. If you roll right, the line will turn left.

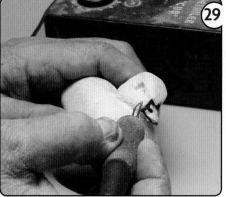

(29)

I start woodburning by using the side of the burning tip to iron in the bill-to-head line, and the sharp edge to make the nostrils and separate the upper and lower bills. I recommend the Detailer Cub by Colwood Industries. I have had this burner for more than 20 years and it is still going strong.

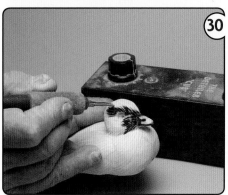

(30)

Start burning in the pin feathers by making short, irregular lines that follow the flow direction you penciled in earlier. Please pay close attention to the eye line. Feathers ahead of the eye go in separate directions, but they merge and flow in the same direction behind the eye.

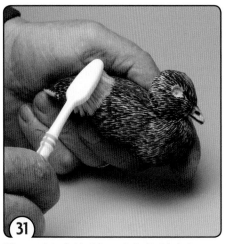

(31)

When you have finished the entire body with the burner, give the whole thing a good scrubbing with an old toothbrush. This will remove loose char from the cuts.

**Apply basecoat**

(32)

Use your old toothbrush to apply the flat white primer. In this case, I'm using gesso, which is a grounding-medium for acrylic paint. The flat white spray we have used on previous lures would work equally well here. I wanted to show you another option for this step. Don't coat the eyeholes.

**Install jig hooks**

(33)

Now is the time to install the hooks. These have to go in before we can paint, so be really careful from here on out. Notice we have simply tacked in the hooks with five-minute epoxy. Just a few spots here and there will do.

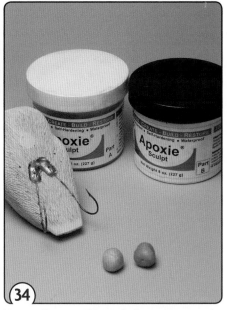

(34)

Mix a small amount of Apoxie Sculpt—a $^{50}/_{50}$ epoxy/putty that is water soluble until it sets. The easiest way to correctly mix it is to make a small ball of each part and roll them together. You have at least 1 to 1½ hours to work it, so don't panic on the time to get it done.

fishy fact

Try fishing rattles for pike—they'll investigate the noise.

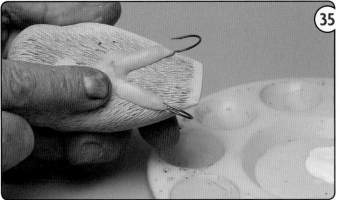

**35** Roll out a small snake of putty and work it into the hook holes. Directly below the lure, I have some clean water (Yeah, I know you can't see it!). Use water on your fingertips to smooth the putty right out.

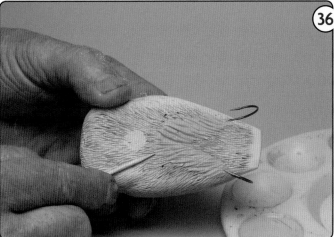

**36** Dip a toothpick in the water and start to texture the putty. The putty will not stick to your tools if they are wet. Please notice the marks are done in the same manner as the burned lines and we are still following the flow. As you work the putty, it is very easy to remove excess. Let the putty cure overnight, and then give the belly a good coat of flat white.

**37** While we were doing the hooks, I used a little of the same putty to semi-fill the eyeholes. I use the 3-D lure eyes, so this step gives the proper depth for that type of eye. You would not need to do this with glass taxidermy eyes.

**Float test**

**38** The last step before the paint is to test this bad boy. Fill the sink with water and drop him in on his back. He should flip right over and float like you see here. Dry him off with a paper towel and get ready to paint.

### Apply yellow undercoat

**(39)** Let's paint this lure the old-fashioned way. Hand brushes and acrylics will allow us the chance to use a different technique. Start with yellow oxide and mix about 1 part paint to roughly 5 to 6 parts water. Use this paint with a flat fan brush and make the lure look like it has yellow chicken-pox. Use your hair dryer to completely dry this coat.

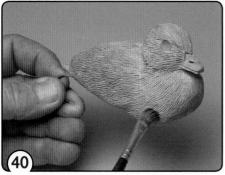

**(40)** Continue painting these pox spots all over the bird in a random fashion. Paint the bill a solid yellow. This is the third coat of spots, and we are starting to get the soft feather look. The reason we are using the spot method is it produces a soft multi-tone paint automatically.

## Dry that paint

When painting with acrylic washes, you must dry every coat every time. If you do not, the second coat will wash off the first one or they will flow together and form a solid color, which is not what we want.

### Create dark areas

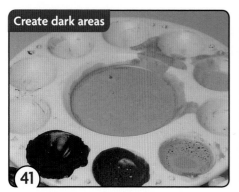

**(41)** Mix some raw sienna with the original yellow oxide to achieve the color on the right. Next, mix some raw sienna with some burnt sienna to achieve the middle color. The color on the left is mostly burnt sienna with a little black to produce a rich dark brown.

**(42)** Water down the brown paint with six parts water. Use the blotch method to block in the dark areas of the color pattern: the top of the head, back, sides, and wing bar. Make sure to leave a yellow eye on both rear flanks. Apply three coats, drying between each.

fishy fact

**For musky, try water 2' to 6' (.6m to 2m) deep with both plants and rocks.**   143

**Paint details**

**43** Change to a size 0 script liner. For this step you will want the full-strength brown mix, with only enough water to let the paint flow off the brush. I'm doing two separate things here: shading in a dark area below the cheek, and painting little feather splits into the rear of the cheek.

**44** Using the script liner, make a series of short, overlapping lines in a random pattern over the brown areas. This will add some softness to the color tone. Here, the right side has been done, but not the left. Can you see the difference?

**45** Water down some raw sienna paint with about 10 parts water. Use this thin mix to wash the entire duck with the flat fan brush. Dry it. Give only the yellow areas a second coat; dry thoroughly. This step ties the colors together—no hard brush lines.

**46** Water down some burnt sienna with 10 parts water and wash the bill. You want a slightly tinted yellow. Load your fine-point brush with dark-brown mix and paint the egg tooth in the front of the bill. Dry the head.

**Clearcoat the bill**

**47** Coat the bill with one to two coats of clear fingernail polish. Keep in mind that you want the bill to look like leather, not glass. While this entire brush painting style is a real pain, the bird looks soft and natural.

## Apply finishing touches

(48) Now is the time to install the eyes. I use the gold 3-D lure eyes because this is a lure and I want a little contrast. Real ducklings have dark brown eyes, but I want those fish to be able to see them, so I use the gold—and they don't look too out of place.

(49) Give the lure two light coats of clear spray. We do not want the duck to look shiny, so you have two options: use gloss from about 24" (610mm) away (sort of painting with a fog), or get clear matte spray. Personally, I'm too cheap to buy a second can just for ducks.

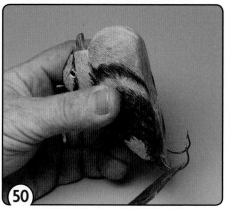

(50) Use a pocketknife, or the like, to clean the excess paint from the hook shanks. The acrylic and clear come off the steel hooks quite easily.

(51) Lay out the hardware. The flat washer at the line tie keeps the screw from gouging the lure's chest. I like brass blades because duckling feet are yellow. Install; make sure the blades are curved surface forward.

## Install hardware

(52) Here is our young duckling, looking pretty darned good, if I do say so myself.

## LURE 11
# Weasel

This weasel lure is another very different model. I designed this lure from a **purchased rough-cut** specifically for large Northern pike and musky; however, it should be equally effective for saltwater predator fish that like to prey on swimming mammals. I like to make this weasel in a natural summer color pattern, which is brown and white, using my **airbrush**. We will be experimenting with a new effect and making wooden fur on this guy with **sawdust**. This lure will fall into the crawler category.

# Weasel Pattern

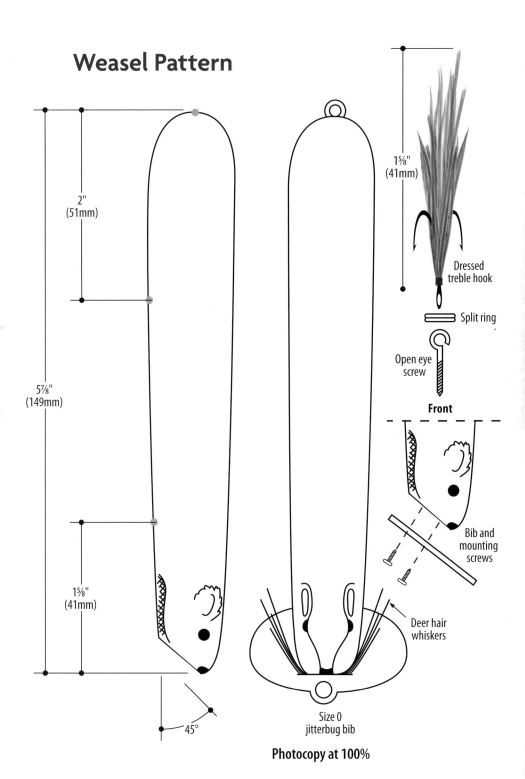

2"
(51mm)

5⅞"
(149mm)

1⅝"
(41mm)

45°

1⅝"
(41mm)

Dressed
treble hook

Split ring

Open eye
screw

**Front**

Bib and
mounting
screws

Deer hair
whiskers

Size 0
jitterbug bib

**Photocopy at 100%**

# Materials and tools list

## Materials
- 6" (152mm) musky stick
- 3-D lure eyes

## Hardware
**Front assembly:**
- Bib and mounting screws

**Belly assembly:**
- 4 open eye screws
- 4 split rings
- 4 dressed treble hooks (See page 163)

## Tools
- Band saw
- Pencil
- Flexible ruler
- Power carver and ruby bit
- Carving knife and homemade sanding rods (optional)
- Sandpaper
- Utility knife
- Prick punch
- Handheld power drill
- ⅛" (3mm) drill bit
- ¹⁄₁₆" (2mm) drill bit
- 5-minute epoxy
- Fine point permanent ink marker
- Split-ring pliers

## Finishing supplies
- Wood glue of choice
- Sawdust from the band saw
- Toothpicks
- Paper plate
- Flat white spray primer
- Airbrush
- Acetone
- Lacquer paints: burnt sienna, black umber, cover white
- Clear spray finish
- Natural-colored buck tail hair
- Clear fingernail polish
- Cotton thread

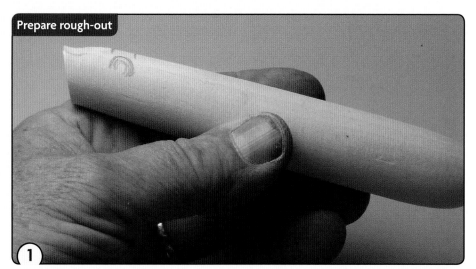

**Prepare rough-out**

**1**

We are going to start this lure with a purchased rough-out that is called a 6" (152mm) musky stick. Make the narrow end the head. Cut the face for the bib and sand a small dip at the top of the nose. The bib cut is also 90° to the long axis of the lure body. Draw in half-circle ears, as high up as the body will allow and ½" to ⅝" (13mm to 16mm) back from the nose.

## Shape the body

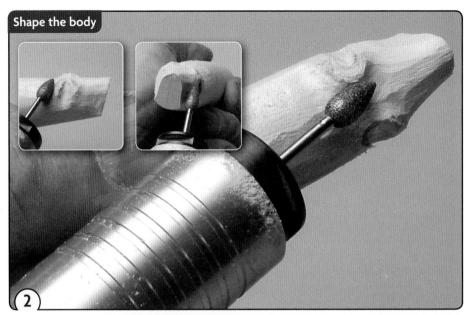

2

I'm using the power carver and a ruby bit to rough in the ears. First, outline the ears; then remove the head around them. Remove wood from the center of the ear. This carving can also be done with your carving knife and small homemade sanding rods. Note the bell shape that results on the front view.

3

Use a light touch to smooth out the center of the ear holes. Weasels have hair inside their ears so don't go too deep, just enough to define this area.

4

Now we smooth the head and ears by using handheld sandpaper. Round and blend all the carving marks into a smooth surface. This shaping and blending does not need to be perfect because when we get to the fur, a lot of the fine detail will be covered up.

## Prepare for eyes and whiskers

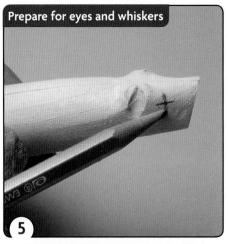

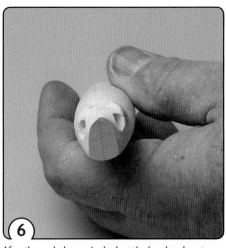

**5** Use a brad-point drill bit to drill the eyeholes. This is not an exact science, but generally you want them about two-thirds the distance from nose to ear. Weasels have small eyes, but I make them bigger to help attract predatory fish. Make the eyes as big as you like 'em.

**6** After the eyeholes are in, look at the lure head-on to check for symmetry. Here you can see that the right side of the nose needs to be brought down a little.

**7** Use your utility knife to carve small slots from the face back toward the cheeks. This is where we will place the lure's whiskers. These slots should run downward at about a 50° to 60° angle.

## Mark and drill pilot holes

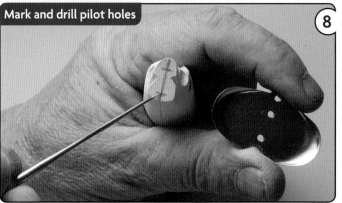

**8** Use the actual bib to mark your centerline for the mounting screw location. Remember that these are fairly small, so use the prick punch to make them. Try to keep these pilot holes 90° to the face angle, not the lure body.

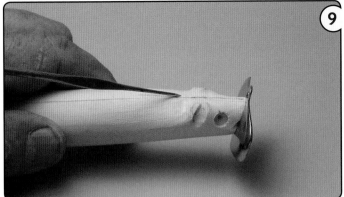

**9** Dry fit the bib to the face and check to see that it is, in fact, 90° to the body. Correct any misalignment by carving or sanding wood from the high side until the bib is square. Notice how the whisker slots look with the bib installed.

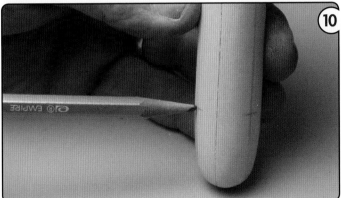

**10** Here we have placed a centerline at the upper edge of the belly line. There needs to be another one on the other side as well. Notice that this locates the four hooks so they will be on the sides of the belly. The head is at the top of this picture.

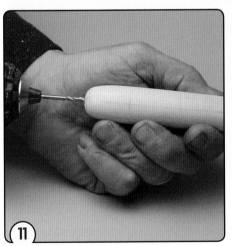

**11** At this point we will drill in the tail hole. This is not a pilot hole—use a ⅛" (3mm) drill bit. Remember to secure the lure in a bench vise if you don't feel comfortable holding it by hand.

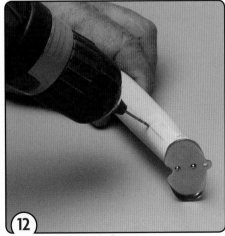

**12** Drill in your pilot holes for the hook mounting eye screws with a ⅟₁₆" (2mm) bit.

fishy fact

**Sharpen your hooks—dragging through rocks and weeds equals dull!**

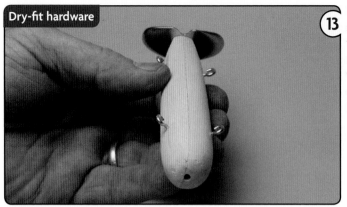

Dry-fit hardware

**13** Dry fit your four hook eye screws and check to see that they line up; they don't need to be perfect, but you want the angles similar to each other so the lure will not roll over on its side.

Create wooden fur

## Don't push it!

If you push on the lure with, say, your fingers, the heavy glue/sawdust coat will slip and leave ridges and bare spots. That result requires you to wash off the entire lure and start over—so don't do it!

**14** Gather the supplies for adding fur to the lure. Start by covering the lure with a good coat of wood glue. I use Tite-Bond. Do not get glue on the face—the mating surface where the bib meets the face needs to be smooth and even.

**15** Holding the weasel by the eyeholes so you do not wipe glue off the body, simply drop the lure into the sawdust and sprinkle some more on top until all the glue is covered. Once that is done, very gently roll the lure in more sawdust.

**16** Notice that I have installed a long eye screw as a handle—you can also do this before applying the glue. Place four toothpicks into the hook screw pilot holes. If you don't do this now, you're in for a real treat finding them later on.

17 Stand the weasel on his toothpick legs or hang him up. After drying overnight (at least 12 hours), gently rub your hand over the body and allow excess fur to fall off. Now spray the lure with a couple of coats of flat white primer.

## Watch the name

Different manufacturers make paints with the same name, but not the same color value. Please notice that the lacquer burnt sienna is dark brown, whereas the acrylic burnt sienna is more reddish.

### Apply basecoats

18 Prepare the usual ratio of burnt sienna lacquer. Set the fan to medium-wide. Spray a light coat on the upper two-thirds of the body. Keep the brown paint above the hook mounting holes. Notice that burnt sienna sprayed lightly produces a tan color.

19 Repeat this step by working down from the back and stopping short of the first coat. We are creating a shading effect so the back is dark and gets lighter as you near the belly.

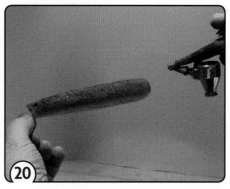

20 Repeat with a third coat, and you can see the rich brown color start to develop.

Try adding salt to your freshwater lure scent.

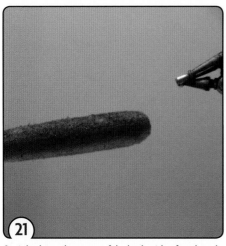

**Paint back and belly**

**21** Go right down the center of the back with a fourth and final coat of the sienna.

**22** Mix a small batch of black umber in the 1:2 ratio and set the spray fan to a thin line. Always check your fan settings on the cardboard before you shoot the lure. Spray a thin black line down the center of the back.

**23** Turn the lure around and darken the top of the head down to approximately the mid-cheek line.

**24** Clean out the brush thoroughly and load in a batch of cover white, mixed in the standard 1:2 ratio. Paint in the belly to sharpen the contrast next to the brown fur. There is no need to paint right up to the brown; just make a nice bright white strip down the center of the belly.

**Apply details**

**25** Use the white to shade in the center of the ears. Apply lightly, because all we want to do is accent the center of the ear. While we did not want any fur on the bib mounting surface, I have freely painted it. The paint will not affect the fit of the bib, but does help to protect the wood.

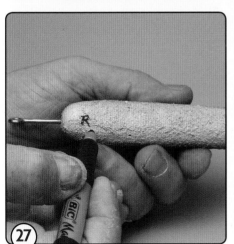

**26** Mix a small amount of 5-minute epoxy and put a small dab into the center of each eyehole. Use the prick punch to install red eyes for a sharp contrast. In reality, weasels have nearly black eyes.

**27** As far as the signature goes, you will find it very difficult to write on the fur. There are two ways to handle this problem: either cut a small flat part of fur off the body, or just initial the lure. Set the ink with two puff coats of clear spray and let dry for 20 minutes.

**28** Now spray the entire lure with two to three coats of clear. We do not want the weasel really shiny, so fog the clear coat on from about 2' (610mm) away. Please remember to let the lure cure for 24 hours before proceeding.

fishy fact

Rub your hands with sugar to keep the smell of gas off your lures.

## Create tail

**29** When the lure is cured, cut some natural-colored buck tail hairs about 2" to 3" (51mm to 76mm) long. Use your fingers to hold these in a rough cylindrical shape and hand wrap about ¼" (6mm) of the butt end with thread. Plain cotton thread will do. Soak the thread in clear fingernail polish and set aside for a few minutes.

**30** Mix some 5-minute epoxy and put a fair amount into the tail holes using a toothpick. Insert the tied end of the tail hair into the hole and set it to the length you think looks right. Weasels have relatively short tails.

## Create whiskers

**31** Put some epoxy into the whisker slots. Place two to three buck tail hairs at a time and vary the angles to make them fan out. Real weasel whiskers are pretty short, but I like to make mine longer, like cat whiskers. The fish like it this way and it looks good as well.

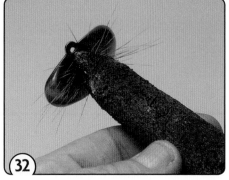

**32** While the epoxy is still soft, I like to install the bib. This makes a good seal of the wood and bib and also ensures the whiskers will stay put. Just before you tighten the bib screws all the way, use the prick punch to straighten any wayward whiskers.

(33) Lay out the hardware and then install it. I use the handle of the prick punch to turn the eye screws in.

## How many hooks?

This four-hook weasel is more of a presentation type. It will fish very well as-is, but if I made this strictly for big game fishing, it would only have two hooks and they would be located right down the center of the belly. This would eliminate any chance of the hooks hanging-up on each other.

### Install hooks

(34) Use your split-ring pliers to install the split rings on either the screws or the hooks. I usually install the screws first, because that way I minimize the possibility of hooking myself. I use natural-colored buck tail dressed treble hooks. Before you decide to hang me, Chapter 3 will show you how to dress your own hooks (see page 163).

(35) Here is Mr. Weasel, all ready to go for a swim. Notice the dressed hooks fairly resemble legs and the dressing will make them wiggle like a swimming animal.

# Options

In this chapter, I would like to cover some optional ideas and additional methods that will help you make more and better types of lures. I will show you how to make jointed bodies, wire-through lures, and dressed hooks, as well as some alternate uses for common hardware items. You really cannot have too many options when it comes to designing fishing lures. I hope these step-by-step procedures give you ideas for designs you would like to try and the confidence to make them. If you learn nothing else from this book, please always have fun with this whole thing.

# Jointed Lures

Let's get started by making a jointed lure. Any lure can be jointed so this is always an option. A jointed lure will create more movement during retrieve, which makes the lure look more like live bait.

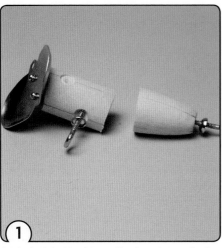

**1** Cut the body into two pieces. The shorter you make the tail section, the faster the wiggle, likewise the longer you make it, the slower it will wiggle.

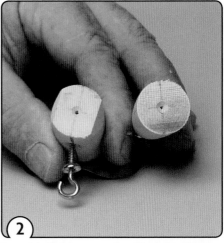

**2** On each half, draw a centerline (North-South) and mark the middle of it. Then use your countersink bit to chamfer a pocket into which an eye screw head can nest.

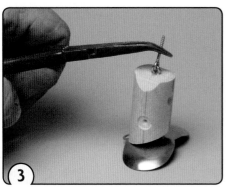

**3** Join two eye screws together. Put 5-minute epoxy into the nest of one of the lure halves and run a screw home. Make sure the epoxy does not fill up the eye, and that it is aligned North-South.

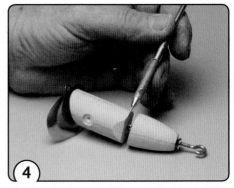

**4** After the epoxy has set, hold the unused eye screw with a small pair of bent needle-nose pliers. Run the second eye screw home by turning the lure body onto it. Orient this eye 90° to the first one (in this case, that would be East to West). Epoxy the second nest as you did the first one.

# Wire-Through Lures

A wire-through lure is much more secure than a non-wired variety. Use the technique to make extra-strong lures. A fish could bite the wood to pieces but that wire and the hooks are still attached to your rod.

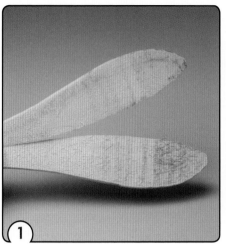

**1**

Cut out a standard-type minnow body from ¾" (19mm) scrap wood. Once the body is cut out, rip it lengthwise. Cut right down the middle of the back from head to tail. Do not sand the inner surfaces smooth. The rough tooth marks left by the saw blade work great for indexing the two halves back together.

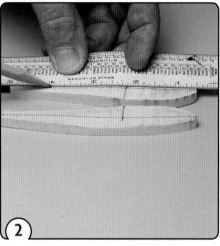

**2**

Draw a centerline down the middle of the insides of the lure body. Start at the center of the head and go to the center of the tail. Draw in the belly hook wire by measuring rearward from the nose (both halves) to wherever that location needs to be and scribing a line 90° to the long centerline.

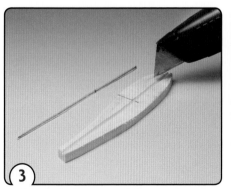

**3**

Use the utility knife to make a shallow V cut down the length of the centerline on both lure halves. This forms the channel for the wire.

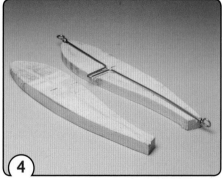

**4**

Make sure to cut the channel for the belly hook loop. This will be wider than the first channel. Now form your wire to fit the pattern of the cuts, starting at the looped end. When it all looks good, form a loop at the other end of the wire.

**5** Epoxy both halves of the lure body and lay the wire into one of the halves. Make sure you have enough epoxy to set the wire and glue both halves together. You want it to ooze out all the way around.

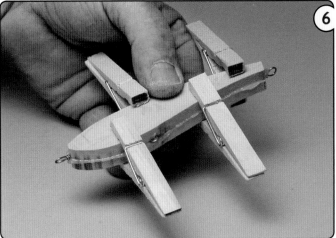

**6** I use my modified clothespins to clamp the body together, but you can also use rubber bands. As the two halves come into contact with each other, the saw tooth marks will align themselves and make it quite easy to get a perfect alignment.

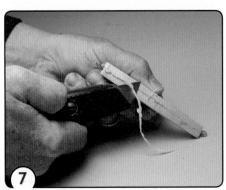

**7** When the epoxy has set, but not fully cured, (it is firm but not rock hard) trim off the excess with your utility knife. This saves plugging-up a lot of sandpaper.

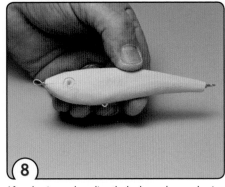

**8** After shaping and sanding the body, you have a classic minnow pattern that is tough as nails.

# Natural-Colored Dressed Treble Hook

Dressing a hook disguises the barbs and turns an artfully placed hook into a wiggling leg, a trailing tail, or anything else you can imagine. This particular dressed hook will be in one of my favorite color patterns: black center surrounded with natural (brown and white) buck tail.

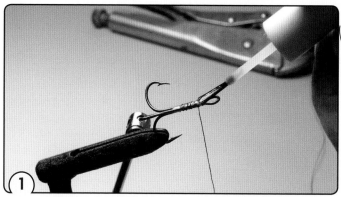

Half-hitch knot.

1. Mount the treble hook in the vise. Notice the hook is initially oriented with the soldered barb down. Fly-tying vises are available from about $9 to $50 plus. Mine is a $9 version, and it's plenty good enough. Start by winding the thread over itself for a few turns and securing with a single half-hitch knot. Use clear fingernail polish to coat this initial wrap.

2. Cut a small bunch of black deer tail. Because we want this lure to be light and airy, just a few hairs will do. Pinch the hairs together and use the hook to measure the length you want. Measure just short of the hook's eye. Wrap the hair on lightly, with just enough thread to hold it in place. Give this wrap a light coat of nail polish.

3. Cut some natural hairs. Use about twice the amount as you used for the black. Try to get an even mix of brown and white, but don't get too fussy. Use the hook to measure the natural hair. Make it short of the eye to a little short of the end of the black. Cut to the proper length by trimming the heavy or fat ends of the hair. Never cut the thin ends unless the pattern calls for it.

**4** Tie this batch of natural hair right on top of the black. Use just a few wraps and very little pressure on the thread. Notice in the photo how the hair is still lying flat. Secure with a half hitch.

**5** Rotate the hook by one barb in either direction. Cut your second batch of natural hair in the same amount as the first. Measure this batch as you did the first group. Tie it on with just enough pressure to hold it in place, and secure with a half hitch. Repeat for the third batch.

**6** Give the entire head a good coating of the nail polish. I use clear, but you could also use red or black. Wrap the head with more thread, putting more tension on the thread. The natural hair will start to bush right out.

**7** Notice those hairs going into the hook eye? We have a way of dealing with those troublemakers. Use a small pair of scissors to trim back the majority of the offending hair. Use the prick punch to rearrange any of the hair that may need it by combing through.

# Colorful Dressed Treble Hook

This colorful hook dressing, which uses both hair and feathers, works well for catching blue gill and crappie.

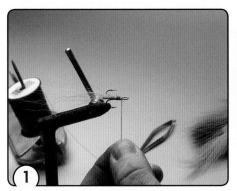

Orient your hook with the soldered barb downward. Cut a few long bright pink hairs and secure them with a few wraps of black cotton thread and a half hitch. Rotate the hook one position and repeat. Repeat for the third batch. Give the head a coat of nail polish.

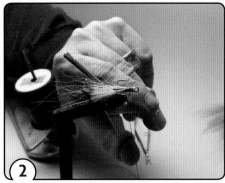

At this point we are going to trim the hair on the thin end. You might think I lied to you before—well, not really, because in this case we want a full body that is relatively short. Please notice the body is about two hook lengths long.

**3** Get out two golden pheasant neck feathers and tie them so they are about twice as long as the pink hair. The type of feathers are not as important as the color and that they be long and thin. Trim the feathers at the head end.

**4** Our next step is to cut a small bunch of lime-green hair about as long as the feathers are. Tie the lime-green hair right on top of the feathers, but do not finish-wrap the head of the hook. Use the prick punch to straighten and align the hair as needed.

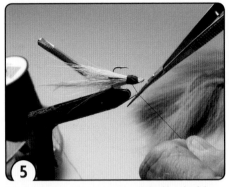

**5** Attach and straighten a second and third batch of the lime-green hair. Because of the full body underneath the batches, the lime-green hair should go all of the way around the hook. Now finish-wrap the head and secure with two half-hitch knots.

**6** Here's another way to deal with the problem hair interfering with the hook eye: Simply heat the end of your prick punch and burn the hair away. It's so easy it ought to be criminal!

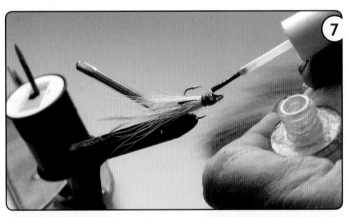

**7** Give the head several coats of nail polish to finish it off.

Here are a few examples of dressed buck-tail hooks. You can use any color combinations you want to, but the process remains the same.

# Alternate Ways to Utilize Hardware

There will be times when you will want to use these alternate methods, either just for the look or to solve some design problem. Never be afraid to think about hardware in unusual or unique ways.

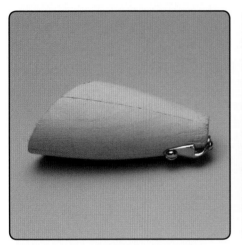

You can use a surface lure hook-hanger as a line tie, instead of an eye screw. This effectively limits the line from being able to move upward. Hook-hangers may also be used to mount rear hooks (shown). Use this when you don't want the hook to be able to swing forward.

If you mount a diving lip backward, the lure will climb when retrieved instead of diving. This arrangement will still cause the lure to wiggle, but it just won't dive.

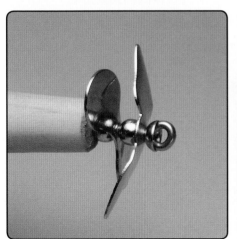

An extra-long eye screw will allow you to mount twin propellers to a lure on the front or rear. By using two different shapes of props you can alter the sound impulse the lure produces in the water.

This photo shows three different ways to utilize cup washers. On the left is a nested cup washer, in the middle is a surface mounted version, and on the right is an inverted version.

fishy fact

**Bump a submerged lure against logs and grass to get fishes' attention.**

# Appendix: Bonus Patterns

In an effort to keep you busy, I would like to include some
bonus patterns for your consideration. I hope that you
will use these as they are, or better yet, make changes and
improvements and design some lures of your individual liking.

## Keel-Weighted Prop, Diver, or Chaser

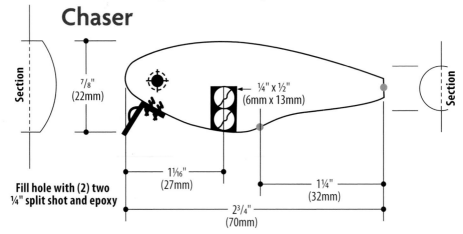

Section

$^7/_8$"
(22mm)

¼" x ½"
(6mm x 13mm)

Section

**Fill hole with (2) two
¼" split shot and epoxy**

1$^1/_{16}$"
(27mm)

1¼"
(32mm)

2$^3/_4$"
(70mm)

**Photocopy at 100%**

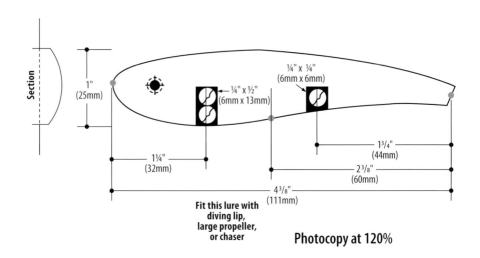

Section

1"
(25mm)

¼" x ¼"
(6mm x 6mm)

¼" x ½"
(6mm x 13mm)

1¼"
(32mm)

1$^3/_4$"
(44mm)

2$^3/_8$"
(60mm)

4$^3/_8$"
(111mm)

**Fit this lure with
diving lip,
large propeller,
or chaser**

**Photocopy at 120%**

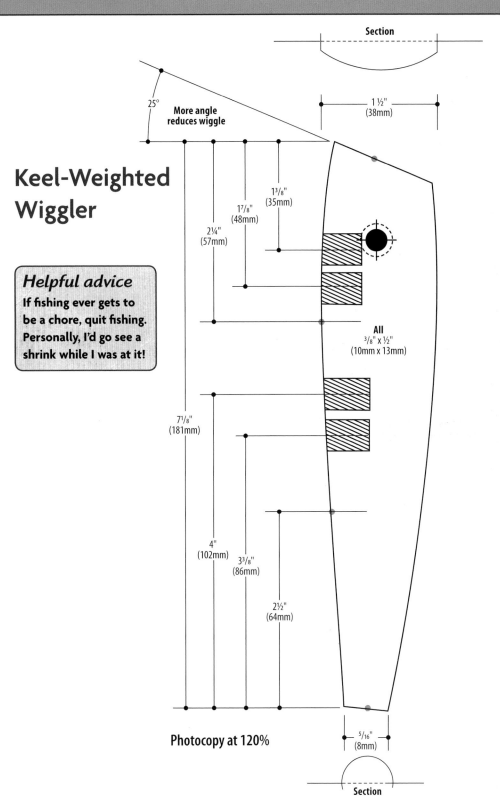

**Section**

25°

**More angle
reduces wiggle**

1½"
(38mm)

# Keel-Weighted
# Wiggler

1³/₈"
(35mm)

1⁷/₈"
(48mm)

2¼"
(57mm)

**All**
³/₈" x ½"
(10mm x 13mm)

7¹/₈"
(181mm)

4"
(102mm)

3³/₈"
(86mm)

2½"
(64mm)

Photocopy at 120%

⁵/₁₆"
(8mm)

**Section**

# Head Knocker
# Floater-Diver

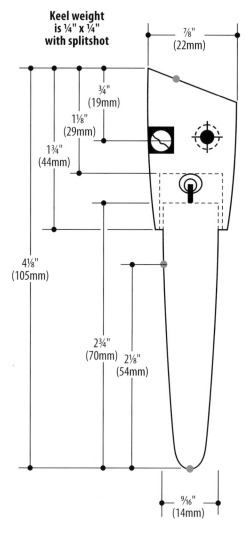

**Keel weight
is ¼" x ¼"
with splitshot**

⅞"
(22mm)

¾"
(19mm)

1⅛"
(29mm)

1¾"
(44mm)

4⅛"
(105mm)

2¾"
(70mm)

2⅛"
(54mm)

⁹⁄₁₆"
(14mm)

**Photocopy at 100%**

## *Safety calling*
**Remember that, for
your own safety, cell
phones and fishing do
not play well together.**

# Prop Bait 1

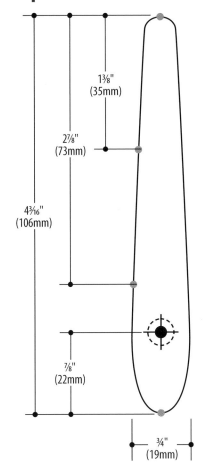

1⅜" (35mm)

2⅞" (73mm)

4³⁄₁₆" (106mm)

⅞" (22mm)

¾" (19mm)

# Prop Bait 2

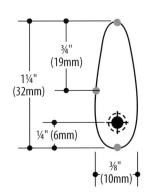

¾" (19mm)

1¼" (32mm)

¼" (6mm)

⅜" (10mm)

# Prop Bait 3

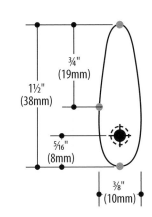

¾" (19mm)

1½" (38mm)

⁵⁄₁₆" (8mm)

⅜" (10mm)

# Prop Bait 4

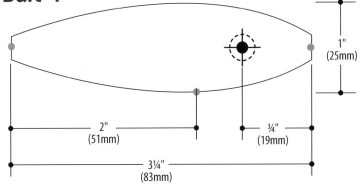

1" (25mm)

2" (51mm)

¾" (19mm)

3¼" (83mm)

**Photocopy at 100%**

# Panfish Prop

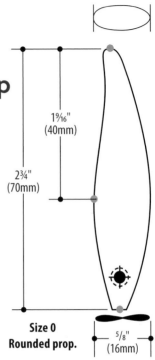

1⁹⁄₁₆"
(40mm)

2¾"
(70mm)

**Size 0
Rounded prop.**

⁵⁄₈"
(16mm)

# Panfish Diver

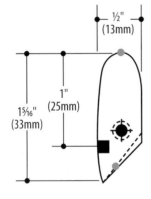

½"
(13mm)

1"
(25mm)

1⁵⁄₁₆"
(33mm)

**⅛" (3mm) Keel
Weight**

*Check the drag*

Before you start to fish, always check your drag, as they have a tendency to stick. You never know if that big guy will be your first fish, and if you get broken-off because you did not check your drag, you're going to be in a mood to expand your vocabulary.

# Bug

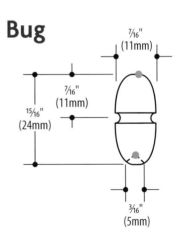

⁷⁄₁₆"
(11mm)

⁷⁄₁₆"
(11mm)

1⁵⁄₁₆"
(24mm)

³⁄₁₆"
(5mm)

**Photocopy at 100%**

# Crawler 1

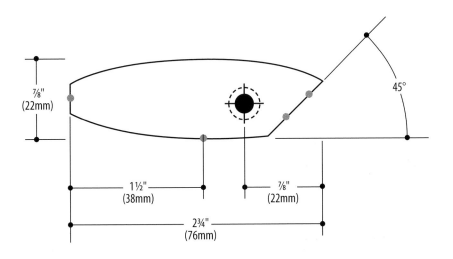

7⁄8"
(22mm)

1½"
(38mm)

7⁄8"
(22mm)

2¾"
(76mm)

45°

# Crawler 2

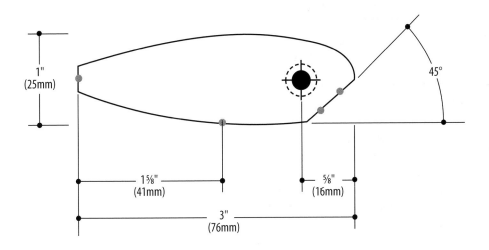

1"
(25mm)

1⁵⁄8"
(41mm)

5⁄8"
(16mm)

3"
(76mm)

45°

**Photocopy at 100%**

# Resources

**Jann's Netcraft Fishing Tackle**
3350 Briarfield Blvd
Maumee, OH 43537
800-638-2723
*www.jannsnetcraft.com*

**Poor Boy's Baits/LureCraft**
513 West Central Avenue
LaGrange, IN 46761
800-925-9088
*www.lurecraft.com*

**Van Dyke's Taxidermy Supply**
PO Box 278
Woonsocket, SD 57385
800-843-3320
*www.vandykestaxidermy.com*

# Index

Note: **Bold** page numbers indicate projects.

## Book staff:
**Acquisitions editor:** Peg Couch
**Designer:** Dan Clarke
**Editor:** Kerri Landis
**Project photographer:** Scott Kriner
**Proofreader:** Lynda Jo Runkle
**Indexer:** Jay Kreider

## Management:
**President:** Alan Giagnocavo
**Vice President,
Sales and Marketing:** Paul McGahren
**Editorial Director:** John Kelsey
**Creative Director:** Troy Thorne

# More Great Books from Fox Chapel Publishing

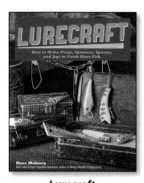

**Lurecraft**
ISBN 978-1-56523-780-3 **$19.99**

**Cooking Fish & Game**
ISBN 978-1-896980-77-5 **$12.99**

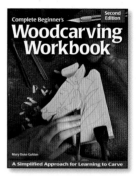

**Complete Beginner's
Woodcarving Workbook**
ISBN 978-1-56523-745-2 **$12.99**

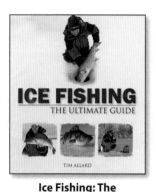

**Ice Fishing: The
Ultimate Guide**
ISBN 978-1-896980-72-0 **$24.99**

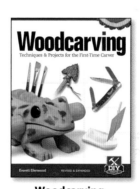

**Woodcarving,
Revised and Expanded**
ISBN 978-1-56523-800-8 **$14.99**

**The Little Book of Whittling**
ISBN 978-1-56523-772-8 **$12.95**

## WOODCARVING ILLUSTRATED    SCROLLSAW woodworking & CRAFTS

In addition to being a leading source of woodworking books and DVDs, Fox Chapel also publishes two premiere magazines. Released quarterly, each delivers premium projects, expert tips and techniques from today's finest woodworking artists, and in-depth information about the latest tools, equipment, and materials.

### Subscribe Today!
*Woodcarving Illustrated:* **888-506-6630**
*Scroll Saw Woodworking & Crafts:* **888-840-8590**
www.FoxChapelPublishing.com

## Look for These Books at Your Local Bookstore or Specialty Retailer